POLICIES AND PROCEDURES MANUAL FOR ACCOUNTING AND FINANCIAL CONTROL

Douglas W. Kurz
General Practice Partner
Coopers & Lybrand

and

Dawn K. Rhodes
General Practice Manager
Coopers & Lybrand

PRENTICE HALL
Paramus, New Jersey 07652

Library of Congress Cataloging-in-Publication Data

Kurz, Douglas W.
    Policies and procedures manual for accounting and financial
control / Douglas W. Kurz, Dawn K. Rhodes.
        p.   cm.
    Includes bibliographical references and index.
    ISBN 0-13-681180-9
    1. Accounting.   2. Corporations—Accounting.   I. Rhodes, Dawn K.
II. Title.
HF5635.K95   1992   91-47164
657—dc20   CIP

Printed in the United States of America

10   9   8   7   6   5   4   3

10   9   8

ISBN 0-13-681180-9   ISBN 0-13-020879-5 (cd-rom)

9 780136 811800   9 780130 208798

PRENTICE HALL
Paramus, NJ 07652
On the World Wide Web at http://www.phdirect.com

DEDICATION

This book is dedicated to Seymour Jones, partner in Coopers & Lybrand (C&L), who was the architect and first National Chairman of C&L's "Emerging Business Services" strategy which proved that a firm the size of C&L could provide both cost effective and superior services to small growing businesses. Sy's hands on, pragmatic client service approach benefited all who worked with him.

ACKNOWLEDGMENTS

Gary Bucciarelli

Peter Collins

Victor V. Coppola

Steve Desloge

Bruce Goldberg

Barbara Hanover

Jerry Karson

James M. Maher

HOW TO USE THIS MANUAL

Using the Material with Minor Changes

An examination of this book might reveal to the potential user that with minor changes the Policy and Procedures Manual and forms could be used as is. This would be especially true of newly formed companies, or existing companies that must either create a new set of Policies and Procedures or greatly modify the existing ones. Under these circumstances, the material might be used as follows:

1. Remove the looseleaf pages of the Policy and Procedures Manual (Part I) and the full-sized forms (Part II).
2. Produce a single working copy of this material.
3. Using the working copy, edit the procedures, if necessary, so as to adapt them to specific requirements.
4. Correct the master (book) copies of the pages. If changes are major, use blank procedure forms from Part II of the book.
5. Produce a working copy of the corrected manual and circulate for review.
6. Retrieve review copies and analyze comments.
7. Coordinate with departments providing conflicting comments.
8. Make changes on the master pages if required.
9. Circulate the masters to secure approval signatures.
10. Insert the company name and/or logo on page one of each policy.
11. Indicate the effective date on page one of each policy.
12. Reproduce (or print), bind and distribute the material on a controlled-copy basis.
13. Maintain and update the material on a continuous basis.

Using the Material for Comparison and Upgrading Purposes

A great number of users of this book will be with organizations which have a long-established set of company policies and procedures. Their purpose in using this book will be to check out their existing systems and upgrade them where required. An approach for doing this might be as follows:

1. Remove the looseleaf pages of the Policy and Procedures Manual (Part I) and the full-sized forms (Part II).
2. Produce a single working copy of this material.

3. On a procedure-by-procedure basis, compare these procedures and forms with existing procedures and forms.

4. Analyze each pair and combine the best of both. Mark up either the existing material or the new material, depending on the amount of changes.

5. Circulate the marked-up copy for comments.

6. Correct existing masters or prepare new ones.

7. Secure approval signatures.

8. Reproduce (or print) and distribute.

9. Maintain and update the material on a continuous basis.

INTRODUCTION

Business failures, fraudulent financial reporting and questionable operating practices have caused the increasing attention on corporate internal controls. Internal control, viewed broadly, encompasses policies and procedures an organization establishes to accomplish a broad range of objectives. Within this broad area of internal control, there are many different subcategories, none mutually exclusive. For example, terms such as operational controls, administrative controls or management controls have been used in the context of improving efficiencies or otherwise controlling business activities, in contrast to accounting controls directed at accurate transactional data recording and reliable financial reporting. A company's procedures established to identify fast-selling products for use in production decisions are an example of the former; its procedures to ensure accurate and complete reporting of sales transactions demonstrate the latter. The categories into which specific internal controls might fall are not particularly important. Far more relevant are the reasons why internal controls are established and the purposes they serve.

Internal controls are put into place largely to allow management to monitor operations, identify business risks and generate pertinent information—both financial and nonfinancial—to drive needed action. In short, controls are designed and implemented so that management can run the business. The nature of controls put into place in any particular organization depends on a number of factors, including its size and complexity, the industry in which it operates, the regulatory and competitive environments and the organizational structure and management philosophy.

It is important to note that internal controls do not—and cannot—guarantee accuracy. They can, however, reduce the risk of misstatements but, for a number of reasons, no system of internal control can ensure accuracy. All internal control systems have limitations, for several reasons:

Costs Versus Benefits

If unlimited resources were available, companies could establish extremely reliable control systems. Redundant checks and balances could provide a very high degree of assurance that information produced by the system is correct. But resources always have constraints, and companies consider, as they must, the relative costs and benefits of establishing internal controls. In determining whether a particular procedure should be performed, the risk of errors and their potential effect are considered alongside the related costs of establishing necessary controls.

Cost-benefit determinations are further complicated depending on the nature of the business activity and changes in technology. Achieving an appropriate balance, and maintaining it in the context of evolving business activities and technology is the objective.

Breakdowns

Even if internal controls are well designed, they may break down. Personnel may misunderstand instructions, make mistakes in judgment or make errors due to carelessness, distraction or fatigue. Temporary personnel performing control duties for vacationing or sick employees might not perform those duties correctly. System changes may be implemented before personnel have been trained to react appropriately to signs of incorrect functioning. There may be collusion between an employee performing an important control function and a customer, supplier or other outside party.

Of particular concern in the current environment is the significant number of corporate restructurings, often the result of leveraged buyouts and frequently accompanied by major reductions in staff levels. Because internal controls depend on the adequacy of supervision and segregation of duties, this may result in increased potential for control breakdowns.

Because costs of controls must be related to their benefits within the context of a company's business and its other controls, and because breakdowns cannot be avoided altogether, the best a company can expect is to have reasonable assurance that material misstatements will not occur or will be detected on a timely basis.

Internal controls are an integral part of a business organization, established primarily for operational purposes and geared to the structure, characteristics, business activities and management of a company. Individual companies must see to it that a control consciousness exists throughout the organization. The consciousness begins, of course, at the very top of the organization and affects the manner in which control procedures are designed and carried out. In particularly well-controlled companies, the boards of directors, or their audit committees, focus on the control environment, especially the tone that top management sets.

In those companies:

- Not only is a comprehensive, written ethics code in place, but the concepts set forth also are emphasized in meetings and everyday actions and communications with company personnel.
- When managers encounter errors or other problems, they do more than just investigate and correct those particular items. The systems that gave rise to (or permitted) the errors are looked at and corrected as needed to prevent similar problems in the future.
- Management recognizes that instructions coming from the top can, however unwittingly, deliver an unintended message. Top management is careful to avoid instructions to subordinates, like "Meet the

budget—I don't care how you do it, just do it," that can be interpreted very differently from the way they were intended.

- Management looks to the audit function as an identification source of needed improvements in control systems.
- Because signals of possible control weaknesses often come from outside the company—from customers and suppliers, for instance—management remains alert to these signals, and mechanisms are in place to facilitate corrective action.

With a positive control environment—including an involved board of directors, a control consciousness on the part of senior management and an effective internal audit function (where the size of the company warrants this function)—the other elements of a company's control structure will likely be well designed and operate effectively.

This manual will focus on one of the initial steps to providing a reliable system of internal control, which is to establish policies and procedures and monitor their compliance.

TABLE OF CONTENTS

How to Use This Manual   v

Introduction   vii

PART I   POLICIES AND PROCEDURES   1

I. Internal Control   3

  1. Effective Systems of Internal Control   5

        1.1   Determination of Validity   7
        1.2   Control of Documents   7
        1.3   Check for Accuracy   7
        1.4   Record in Appropriate Journals   8
        1.5   Check for Completeness   8
        1.6   Investigation of Unprocessed Transactions   8
        1.7   Segregation of Duties   8
        1.8   Performance of Monthly Reconciliations   8
        1.9   Timely Investigation of Differences   8
        1.10 Safeguarding of All Accounting Records   8

II. Controls in an EDP Environment   9

  1. Application Controls   11

        1.1   Completeness of Input   11
        1.2   Accuracy of Input   12
        1.3   Authorization of Transactions   13
        1.4   Handling of Rejected Transactions   13
        1.5   Completeness and Accuracy of Computer-Generated Data/Transactions 14
        1.6   Completeness and Accuracy of Updating   14

  2. System/Program Implementation   15

        2.1   Management of System Development   15
        2.2   System Design   16
        2.3   Vendor-Supplied Packages   16
        2.4   System and Programming Standards   16

2.5	Testing	16
2.6	Cataloging	17
2.7	Documentation	17
2.8	Standing Data Conversion	18
2.9	Transaction Data Conversion	18
2.10	Set-Up of New Data	18
	Figure 2-1 Sample Documentation Index	*19*

3. Program Maintenance — **21**

3.1	Internally Maintained Applications	21
3.2	Vendor Maintained Packages	22
3.3	Cataloging	23
	Figure 3-1 Sample Service Request Form	*24*
	Figure 3-2 Sample Cataloging Authorization Form	*25*

4. Computer Operations — **27**

4.1	Scheduling	27
4.2	Job Set-Up and Execution	27
4.3	Use of Correct Data Files	28
4.4	Operator Actions	28
4.5	Activity Logs	28
4.6	Back-Up and Recovery	29
	Figure 4-1 Sample Operations Schedule	*31*
	Figure 4-2 Sample Operator Incident Log	*32*

5. Security — **33**

5.1	Overall System Access Controls	33
5.2	Security Policy	33
5.3	Security Administration	34
5.4	Dial-Up Access	34
5.5	Physical Access	34
5.6	Custody of Data and Programs Stored Off-Line	34
5.7	Utilities and High-Level Programming Languages	35
5.8	Bypassing Normal Access Controls	35
5.9	Output	35
	Figure 5-1 Sample Access Request Form	*36*

III. General Ledger and Journal Entries   **37**

1. Maintaining an Effective Accounting System   **39**

1.1 General Ledger Set-Up and Posting   39
1.2 Arrangement of Account Titles   40
1.3 Establishment of Contra Accounts   41
1.4 Financial Information Adequacy   41

2. General Ledger Activity   **43**

2.1 Posting Monthly Activity to the General Ledger   43
2.2 Documentation of Journal Entries Not Originating from Journals   44
2.3 Adequate Documentation for All Journal Vouchers   45
2.4 Authorization of Entries   45
2.5 Review of All Authorized Vouchers   45
Figure 2-1 Journal Voucher   *46*

3. Adequate General Ledger Maintenance   **47**

3.1 Preparation of Trial Balance   47
3.2 Performance of Reconciliations   47
3.3 Review of Trial Balance and Reconciliations   47
3.4 Close of Income and Expense Items   48

IV. Cash   **49**

1. Cash Management   **51**

1.1 Maximizing Return on Idle Funds   51
1.2 Expediting of Cash Receipts   51
1.3 Collection Practices   52
1.4 Deferring Disbursements   52
1.5 Cash Budgets   52
Figure 1-1 Short-Term Investment Vehicles   *53*

2. Cash Receipts   **55**

2.1 Opening the Mail   55
2.2 Endorsement of Checks   55
2.3 Bank Deposits   56
2.4 Reconciliation of Cash/Checks Received to Bank Deposit   56
2.5 Summarize Cash Receipts   56

3. Disbursements from Bank Accounts   **57**

   3.1   Preparing Checks and Bank Transfers   57
   3.2   Check Signing   58
   3.3   Disbursement of Checks   58
   3.4   Cancel Supporting Documents   58
   3.5   Maintenance of Check Control Log   59
   3.6   Summarize Cash Disbursements   59
   Figure 3-1   Check Request Form   *60*
   Figure 3-2   Check Control Log   *61*

4. Imprest and Similar Funds   **63**

   4.1   Disbursement of Funds   63
   4.2   Summarize Disbursements   63
   4.3   Reimbursement of Imprest Funds   63
   4.4   Payment of Payroll Through Imprest Funds   64
   4.5   Post Activity to the General Ledger   64

5. Bank Reconciliations   **65**

   5.1   Preparing Bank Reconciliations   65
   5.2   Determination of Reconciling Items   65
   5.3   Review of Bank Reconciliation   66
   Figure 5-1   Bank Reconciliation   *67*

V. Revenue Cycle   **69**

1. Credit Policies   **71**

   1.1   Segregation of Duties   71
   1.2   Customer Credit Check   71
   1.3   Establishment of Credit Guidelines   72
   1.4   Credit Limit Increases   72
   1.5   Accounts Receivable Agings   72
   1.6   Security Interest in Items Sold   72
   1.7   Guidelines for Collection of Delinquent Accounts   72

2. Customer Purchase Orders   **73**

   2.1   Customer Purchase Order Log   73
   2.2   Prenumbered Sales Order Forms   73
   2.3   Credit Department Approvals   74

2.4   Sales Order Form as Requisition for Merchandise   74
2.5   Sales Order Form as Packing Slip   74
2.6   Shipping Log Preparation   75
Figure 2-1   Sales Order Form   76
Figure 2-2   Shipping Log   77

3. Revenue Recognition   79

3.1   Prenumbered Invoices   79
3.2   Invoicing Procedures   79
3.3   Sales Journal Review   79
3.4   Sales Journal Summarization   80
3.5   Sales Journal Posting to General Ledger   80
3.6   Review of Shipping Log or Service Records   80
Figure 3-1   Sales Invoice Form   81

4. Accounts Receivable   83

4.1   Posting Sales Invoices   83
4.2   Posting as an Independent Function   83
4.3   Timely Identification of Errors   83
4.4   Posting of Adjustments   83
4.5   Reconciliation of Accounts Receivable Subsidiary Ledger   84
4.6   Review of Credit Balances   84
4.7   Review of Cutoffs   84

5. Customer Returns and Allowances   85

5.1   Written Authorization   85
5.2   Count and Examination of Returned Goods   85
5.3   Issuance of Credit Memo   85
5.4   Separate Check of Mathematical Accuracy   86
5.5   Authorization of and Conditions for Allowances   86
5.6   Approved Allowances   86
5.7   Review of Credit Memo Numerical Sequence   86
5.8   Valid But Unprocessed Claims   86
Figure 5-1   Credit Memo   87

6. Other Revenues   89

6.1   Rental Income   89
6.2   Royalties   89

6.3	Deferred Income	89
6.4	Barter Transactions	90

VI. Production Cycle | | **91**

1. Sales and Product Forecasts | | **93**

1.1	Preparation of Sales Forecasts	93
1.2	Determination of Production Volume	93
1.3	Review of Production Levels and Related Sales	94

2. Cost-Flow Methods | | **95**

2.1	Determination of Appropriate Method	95
2.2	Consistent Use of Method Selected	95
2.3	Allocation of Production Costs—Overhead Application Rate	96
2.4	Proration of Variance and Under/Over Absorbed Overhead	96
2.5	Variance Analysis	96
2.6	Review of Standard Costs and Overhead Rates	96

3. Inventory Control | | **97**

3.1	Custodial Control of Operations	97
3.2	Written Procedures for Inventory Custody	97
3.3	Authorization for Movement of Inventory	97
3.4	Independent Check of Transferred Items	98
3.5	Reconciliation of Regularly Scheduled Physical Counts	98
Figure 3-1	*Materials Requisition Form*	*99*

4. Perpetual Inventory | | **101**

| 4.1 | Perpetual Inventory Not Used | 101 |
| 4.2 | Opening Inventory Balance | 101 |

5. Periodic Physical Inventory | | **103**

5.1	Proper Control of Physical Inventory	103
5.2	Concurrent Physical Inventories	103
5.3	Frequent Period Physical Counts	104
5.4	Inventory Not on Premises	105
5.5	Inventory Held in Public Warehouses	105

5.6	Proper Identification of Inventory Ownership	105
5.7	Indirect Materials and Supplies Inventory	106
5.8	Reconciliation of Physical to Perpetual Inventory	106
Figure 5-1	*Inventory Tag Example*	*108*

6. Inventory Obsolescence **109**

6.1	Revalue Certain Inventory to Net Realizable Value	109
6.2	Disposal of Obsolete or Excess Inventories	109

7. Perpetual Inventory **111**

7.1	Adjustments to the General Ledger	111
7.2	Physical Count Summary Reviewed for Accuracy	111
7.3	Approval for Posting to General Ledger	111

VII. Prepaid Expenses **113**

1. Monitoring and Accounting for Prepaid Expenses **115**

1.1	Reviewing Incoming Invoices to Ensure Prepayment	115
1.2	Maintenance of Asset Register	115
1.3	Amortization Periods and Rates	116
1.4	Preparation of Standard Journal Entries	116
Figure 1-1	*Asset Register*	*117*

2. Controlling Asset Balances **119**

2.1	Preparation of Reconciliations	119
2.2	Investigation of All Discrepancies	119
2.3	Supervisory Review of the Reconciliation	119

VIII. Investments **121**

1. Investment of Idle Funds **123**

1.1	Investment Policy	124
1.2	Authorization of Investment Vehicles	124
1.3	Authorization of Investments	125
1.4	Investment Purchases	125
1.5	Investment Sales	125

	1.6	Investment Sales Gain or Loss	126
	1.7	Investment Sales Proceeds	126
	1.8	Investment Results Reports	126
	1.9	Reconciliation of Investment Accounts	126
	1.10	Investment Account Balances Agreed to Bank/Broker Statements	126
		Figure 1-1A Investment Control Log—Purchases	*128*
		Figure 1-1B Investment Control Log—Sales	*129*
		Figure 1-2 Investment Purchase/Sale Authorization Form	*130*
		Figure 1-3 Investment Gain/Loss Calculation Worksheet	*131*

2. Safeguarding of Investments **133**

	2.1	Investments Held by Authorized Agent	133
	2.2	Investment Certificate or Safekeeping Receipt	133
	2.3	Investment Control Log	134
	2.4	Physical Safeguards	134
	2.5	Investment Access Control Log	134
	2.6	Investment Storage Facility	134
	2.7	Preparation of Investment File	134
		Figure 2-1 Safekeeping Receipt Form	*136*

3. Return on Investment **137**

	3.1	Interest Income	137
	3.2	Common/Preferred Stock	137
	3.3	Premium/Discount on Bonds and Notes Receivable	138
	3.4	Investment Income Schedule	138
	3.5	Investment Summary Schedule	138
	3.6	Proper Valuation of "Marketable Equity Securities"	138
		Figure 3-1 Interest Income Worksheet	*139*
		Figure 3-2 Dividend Earnings Worksheet	*140*

4. Investments With Significant Influence **141**

| | 4.1 | Equity Method of Accounting | 141 |
| | 4.2 | Investee Corporation Earnings | 141 |

IX. Property, Plant, and Equipment **143**

1. Additions to Property, Plant, and Equipment **145**

| | 1.1 | Approval of Capital Budgeting | 146 |
| | 1.2 | Capital Asset Purchase Authorizations | 146 |

1.3	Approval of Appropriation Requests	146
1.4	Long-Term Lease or Purchase	146
Figure 1-1	*Appropriations Request Form*	*147*

2. Accurate Records of Property, Plant, and Equipment **149**

2.1	Receipt and Identification of Capital Assets	149
2.2	Review of Purchase Price Variances	149
2.3	Maintenance of Detailed Fixed Asset Ledgers	149
2.4	Depreciable Assets Net Acquisition Costs	150
2.5	Posting to Detailed Ledger	150
2.6	Reconciliation to General Ledger	150
2.7	Investigation and Resolution of Differences	150
2.8	Review of Differences	150
2.9	Capitalization of Expenditures While Building	150
2.10	Expenditures—Capitalization vs. Expense	151
Figure 2-1	*Fixed Asset Ledger*	*152*

3. Depreciation of Property, Plant, and Equipment **155**

3.1	Determination of Useful Life	155
3.2	Determination of Depreciation Method	156
3.3	Tax Deferrals Through Accelerated Depreciation Methods	156

4. Existence of Capital Assets **157**

4.1	Identification and Record of Assets	157
4.2	Comparison to Detailed Records	157
4.3	Resolution of Differences	158

5. Disposal of Capital Assets **159**

5.1	Documentation of Disposal	159
5.2	Recording Disposal	159
5.3	Fully Depreciated Assets	160
Figure 5-1	*Disposal Form*	*161*

X. Purchasing Cycle **163**

1. Determination of Needs **165**

1.1	Methods to Determine Needs	165
1.2	Preparation of Requisitions for Routine Goods and Services	166

	1.3	Initiation of Requisitions for Specialized Services	167
	1.4	Initiation of Requisitions for Plant, Property, and Equipment	167
	1.5	Limitation on Purchases Through Imprest Funds	167
	Figure 1-1	*Requisition Form*	*168*

2. Placement of Orders   **169**

	2.1	Capable Purchasing Personnel	169
	2.2	Establishment of Purchasing Guidelines	169
	2.3	Entering Into Purchase Commitments	170
	2.4	Preparation of Prenumbered Purchase Orders	170
	2.5	Reviewing for Accuracy	170
	2.6	Multiple Copy Purchase Order Forms	171
	2.7	Review of Unmatched Purchase Commitments	171
	2.8	Approval of Review	171
	Figure 2-1	*Approval Limit Schedule*	*172*
	Figure 2-2	*Purchase Order*	*173*

3. Receipt and Acceptance   **175**

	3.1	Inspection of All Goods and Services	175
	3.2	Proper Communication Between Departments	176
	3.3	Preparation of Receiving Request	176
	3.4	Receiving Documentation Filed in Receiving and Sent to Purchasing	177
	3.5	Inspection and Approval of All Services Received	177
	3.6	Storing and Controlling of Goods	177
	3.7	Comparison of Receiving Log to Receiving Reports	178
	3.8	Approval and Review of Discrepancies in 3.7	178
	Figure 3-1	*Receiving Report—Description and Quantity Manually Written*	*179*
	Figure 3-2	*Receiving Report—Copy of Purchase Order Used*	*180*
	Figure 3-3	*Receiving Control Log*	*181*

4. Establishment of Accounts Payable   **183**

	4.1	Establishment of Control Devices	183
	4.2	Preparation of the Voucher Package	183
	4.3	Procedures Performed on Voucher Package	184
	4.4	Processing of Freight Bills	184
	4.5	Guidelines for C.O.D. Purchases	185
	4.6	Recording Invoice in the Voucher Register or Purchase Journal	186

4.7	Posting Vendor Invoices to the Accounts Payable Subledger	186
4.8	Reconciliation of A/P Subledger to A/P General Ledger	187
4.9	Review of Debit Balances in Accounts Payable	187
4.10	Reconciliation of A/P Subsidiary Records to Suppliers' Records	187
4.11	Approval and Review of Discrepancies in 4.10	187
	Figure 4-1 Voucher Sheet	*188*

5. Return of Goods to Suppliers — **189**

5.1	Preparation of a Rejection of Material Report	189
5.2	Shipment of Goods Back to Vendor	190
5.3	Preparation of a Debit Memorandum for Returned Goods	190
5.4	Circulation of Debit Memo	191
5.5	Comparison of Original Invoice Price to Debit Memo	191
5.6	Review of Materials Rejection Reports	191
5.7	Receipt of Credit Memorandum from Vendor	192
5.8	Review of Unmatched Credit (Debit) Memorandum	192
5.9	Review and Approval of Discrepancies in 5.7 and 5.8	192
	Figure 5-1 Materials Rejection Report	*193*
	Figure 5-2 Debit Memo	*194*

6. Purchase Cut-Off — **195**

6.1	Procedures for Proper Purchasing Cut-Off at End of Accounting Period	195

XI. Notes Payable and Long-Term Debt — **197**

1. Financial Resource Requirements — **199**

1.1	Notes Payable	199
1.2	Installment and Mortgage Loans	200
1.3	Bonds	200
1.4	Long-Term Leases	201

2. Assumption and Authorization of Debt — **203**

2.1	Board of Directors Resolution	203
2.2	Debt Approval and Agreement	203
2.3	Records and Collateralization of Debt	203

3. Safekeeping of Debt Agreements — **205**

3.1	Original Agreements and Instruments	205
3.2	Physical Safety of Agreements and Instruments	205

4. Record of Debt   207

    4.1   Cash Received in Exchange for Debt   207
    4.2   Property, Plant, and Equipment in Exchange for Debt   207
    4.3   Bond Price Fluctuations   208

5. Timely Interest Expense Accruals   209

    5.1   Interest Accrual Using Amortization Schedule   209
    5.2   Interest Accrual With Amortization Schedule   209

6. Debt Payments   211

    6.1   Separate Principal and Interest Components   211
    6.2   Debt Payment Through General Ledger Distribution   211
    6.3   Debt Payment by Other Method   212

7. Bond Discounts and Premiums   213

    7.1   Bond Amortization Schedule   213
    7.2   Timely Recording of Discounts and Premiums   213

8. Current and Long-Term Debt Summary   215

    8.1   Debt Instrument Activity Summary   215
    8.2   Comparison to General Ledger   215
    8.3   Current Portion of Long-Term Debt   216

9. Debt Covenants   217

    9.1   Debt Covenant Review Checklist   217
    9.2   Frequency of Checklist Preparation   217
    9.3   Noncompliance with Debt Covenants   218

XII. Accrued Liabilities   219

1. Monitoring of Accrued Liabilities   221

    1.1   Establishing List of Expenses   221
    1.2   Preparation of Detailed Register   222
    1.3   When and How Accrued Liabilities Occur   222
    1.4   Recording the Accrual   222
    1.5   Review of the Account Balance   222

2. Reconciliations and Accuracy — **223**

   2.1 Performance of Monthly Reconciliations   223
   2.2 Investigation of Discrepancies   223
   2.3 Supervisory Review of the Reconciliation   223

XIII. Payroll Cycle — **225**

1. Payroll and Personnel/Human Resources — **227**

   1.1 New Employees   227
   1.2 Compensation and Evaluation   228
   1.3 Vacation and Sick Pay   228

2. Wages and Salaries — **229**

   2.1 Changes in Payroll Data   229
   2.2 Authorization of Changes in Payroll Data   229
   2.3 Comparison of Payroll Data to Personnel Files   230
   Figure 2-1 Personnel Action Form   *231*

3. Timekeeping — **233**

   3.1 Maintenance of Time Records   233
   3.2 Overtime Approval   233
   3.3 Reconciliation of Payroll to Supporting Records   233
   Figure 3-1 Time Card   *235*
   Figure 3-2 Employee Time Sheet   *236*

4. Payroll Calculation — **237**

   4.1 Time Cards   237
   4.2 Payroll Compared to Control Totals   237
   4.3 Independent Payroll Calculations   237
   4.4 Payroll Authorization   237

5. Payment to Company Employees — **239**

   5.1 Distribution of Payroll   239
   5.2 Receipt Log for Cash Payments   239
   5.3 Comparison of Employee Check Endorsements to Signatures on File   239

| | 5.4 | Unclaimed Payroll Checks | 239 |
| | 5.5 | Reconciliation of Payroll Bank Accounts | 240 |

6. Payroll Deductions   **241**

	6.1	Recording of Payroll Deductions	241
	6.2	Independent Check of Payroll Deductions	241
	6.3	Review of Payroll Deductions Payments to Third Parties	241

XIV. Capital Stock   **243**

1. Authorization, Issuance, and Maintenance of Capital Stock   **245**

	1.1	Approval by Board of Directors	245
	1.2	Issuance of Certificates	245
	1.3	Transferability of Stock Certificates	246
	1.4	Maintaining Permanent Evidence of Transfer	246
	1.5	Issuance of Stock When Full Payment is Received	246

2. Outstanding Stock Procedures   **247**

	2.1	Maintenance of Stock Journal	247
	2.2	Preparation of Registrar Reports	247
	2.3	Posting to the General Ledger Accounts	248

3. Capital Stock Records   **249**

	3.1	Reconciliation to General Ledger	249
	3.2	Examination of Unissued and Retired Stock Certificates	249
	3.3	Investigation of Discrepancies	249
	3.4	Approval of Reconciliation, Examination, and Investigation	249

PART II   FULL-SIZED FORMS   **251**

   Index of Forms   253

PART III   APPENDICES   **293**

   A. Sample Financial Statements   **295**

ABC Service Company	297
XYZ Retail Company and Subsidiary	301
ACE Manufacturing Corporation	306

B. Key Business Ratios and Other Analytical Measurements   **311**

C. Computer Systems Selection and Implementation   **317**

D. Three-Way Budget—The Aspects of Cash Management   **329**

INDEX   **351**

PART I

POLICIES AND PROCEDURES

The following pages are a compilation of actual policies, procedures, and techniques which should be used in controlling certain business activities. It has been designed to use "as-is" or can be modified, as necessary, to fit your company. Follow the steps as outlined in "How to Use This Manual" to begin realizing the benefits of increased effectiveness and efficiency now!

Section I

INTERNAL CONTROLS

Company Name	Date
Approval	

1. *EFFECTIVE SYSTEMS OF INTERNAL CONTROL*

Policy The company should maintain an effective system of internal control in order to monitor compliance with policies and procedures established by management.

General Internal control can be divided into two areas: accounting controls and administrative controls. Administrative controls deal with the operations of the business, whereas the accounting controls deal with accounting for such operations. This manual focuses on internal accounting controls (although there may be some overlap between the two). Accounting controls should be designed to achieve the five basic objectives:

Validation

Validation is the examination of documentation, by someone with an understanding of the accounting system, for evidence that a recorded transaction actually took place and that it occurred in accordance with the prescribed procedures. As systems grow more sophisticated, validation is a built-in component whereby the transactions test themselves against predetermined exceptions. For example, only goods received are recorded on a receiving report and only goods shipped appear on a shipping report or bill of lading. The vendor's invoice can then be compared to the receiving report and the sales invoice can be compared to the shipping report. Another example confirms that all relevant details of a transaction are properly recorded: the nature, quality, and condition of goods received are checked by counting, weighing, and inspecting and recorded at time of receipt.

Accuracy

The accuracy of amounts and account classification is achieved by establishing control tasks to check calculations, extensions, additions, and account classifications.

The control objective is to be certain that each transaction is recorded at the correct amount, in the appropriate account, in the right time period. For example, one might "double-check" another individual's work on sales invoices by repeating the calculations, extensions, and additions and reviewing the account distributions.

Control tasks, which ensure that transactions are recorded and reported in the proper accounting period, are essential to accurate financial reporting. For example, when goods are received they should be checked and recorded at the time of receipt. The receiving records should then be matched with the related vendors' invoices as a further check on the timely recording of transactions.

Completeness

Completeness of control tasks ensures that all transactions are initially recorded on a control document and accepted for processing once and once only.

Completeness controls are needed to ensure proper summarization of information and proper preparation of financial reports. To ensure proper summarization of recorded transactions as well as a final check of completeness, subsidiary ledgers and journals with control accounts need to be maintained. This is because individual transactions are the source of the ultimate product—financial reports.

Completeness can be achieved by using two techniques. One is to sequentially number all transactions via documents as soon as the transactions occur and then apply the control task of accounting for all the numbered documents completed in the processing. The use of "control totals" also provides information by which control is exercised. This is done by totaling the critical numbers before and after processing. When the two totals agree, one assumes that the processing is complete.

Maintenance

The objective of the maintenance controls is to monitor accounting records after the entry of transactions to ensure that they continue to reflect accurately the operations of the business. The control system should provide systematic responses to errors when they occur, to changed conditions, and to new types of transactions. The maintenance function should be accomplished principally by the operation of the system itself. Control maintenance policies require procedures, decisions, documentation, and subsequent review by a responsible authorized individual. Disciplinary control tasks, such as supervision and segregation of duties, should ensure that the internal control system is operating as planned.

Physical Security

It is important in all business organizations that the assets are adequately protected. Physical security of assets requires that access to assets be limited to authorized personnel. One means to limit access to both assets and related accounting records is through the use of physical controls. Protection devices restrict unauthorized personnel from obtaining direct access to assets or indirect access through accounting records which could be used to misappropriate assets. Locked storage facilities restrict access to inventories, and fireproof vaults prevent access to petty cash vouchers. Transaction recording equipment limits access to assets by limiting the number of employees involved in recording and posting transactions, thereby minimizing the possibility of fraudulent misrepresentation. Electronic cash registers record cash sales both on cash register tapes and at an off-site electronic storage facility, creating two records of a single transaction.

Many control procedures are common to various areas of accounting. They have been discussed in this chapter as a convenience to the user of this manual and to emphasize that similar procedures are applicable to many control objectives.

Associated Materials   None

Procedures   **Determination of Validity**

1.1   All transactions should be reviewed by an informed individual and a determination made as to their validity (i.e., appropriate approvals have been obtained and/or comparisons have been made to the underlying documentation).

Control of Documents

1.2   All transactions should be entered on a control document.
(a) If the document is internally generated it should be prenumbered and physical control should be maintained over unissued documents.
(b) If the document is prepared externally it should be numbered immediately upon receipt, in sequential order.

Check for Accuracy

1.3   Documents supporting transactions should be checked for mathe-

matical accuracy. The individual performing the check should initial or sign the document. The extent of checking can be either:
(a) 100% recalculation or
(b) a check of amounts above (or below) a specified amount.

Record in Appropriate Journals

1.4 As transactions are completed (and/or matched with other supporting documentation), they should be entered into the appropriate journals or registers with a notation or cross-reference indicating the completion of the transactions.

Check for Completeness

1.5 Completeness of the journal or register should be established by reviewing the numerical control of items (established in 1.2) that have not been matched with supporting documentation (if required) or are not complete.

Investigation of Unprocessed Transactions

1.6 Unprocessed transactions should be investigated periodically by a person other than the recordkeeper and corrective action taken.

Segregation of Duties

1.7 An individual, independent of the custodian of the journals generated in 1.4, should establish a separate control account to account for the completed items.

Performance of Monthly Reconciliations

1.8 Reconciliations between subsidiary records and control accounts should be performed monthly to ensure that postings are correct and adjustments have been properly processed.

Timely Investigation of Differences

1.9 All differences should be investigated on a timely basis.

Safeguarding of All Accounting Records

1.10 All assets and the accounting records should be properly safeguarded to prevent theft.

Section II

CONTROLS IN AN EDP ENVIRONMENT

This section provides guidance to those businesses that currently have economic data processing systems in operation. Some businesses, for certain practical reasons, still have not computerized their accounting systems. For those that have not, please read Appendix C, "Computer Systems Selection and Implementation," in the back of the procedures manual.

1. *APPLICATION CONTROLS*

Policy Application controls should be applied to ensure the completeness, accuracy, and validity of data.

General Through a combination of both manual and programmed procedures, each application should include a series of control steps to be followed from the onset of a task through its final disposition. For example, if an account number is rejected by a programmed edit check, manual procedures should be in place to ensure follow-up, correction, and resubmission of the item in question.

Associated Materials None

Procedures **Completeness of Input**

1.1 Completeness of input is concerned with whether or not *all* transactions are recorded. All transactions should be recorded and input into the system once and only once. At least one of the following methods should be used to ensure the completeness of input:

(a) One-for-one checking involves the review of all individual items that have been introduced to or updated in a file. To check for completeness, all documents associated with the input should be compared to a computer-generated listing of all activity for the corresponding file.

(b) Batch or control totals involve the manual separation of input transactions into groups or batches that are to be processed together. Various counts or calculations are then performed on each batch to check for completeness. The following methods should be used for this purpose:

  • A document count entails a manual count of documents within a batch to be entered into the system. Once input, the total number of documents entered should be calculated by the system and compared to the manual count.

- A line count or item count is similar to a document count but involves totaling the number of lines or items that have been entered into the system.

(c) Computer matching entails the use of a master file to identify transactions for which no match exists (e.g., an invoice from a vendor not on the master file) or items expected to match (e.g., purchase orders on file awaiting matching invoices). A history file may also be used to identify duplicate records (e.g., input of a previously paid invoice from a vendor).

(d) A computer sequence check can be implemented to verify the completeness of input when serially ordered documents are used (e.g., invoice numbers, journal entry numbers, transaction batch numbers). The computer can also assign sequential numbers on input for subsequent tracking. The computer should examine the serial numbers associated with the items that have been input and identify missing or duplicate numbers.

Accuracy of Input

1.2 Accuracy of input controls focuses on the data associated with each transaction. All transactions should be recorded and input accurately into the system. At least one of the following methods should be used to ensure the accuracy of input:

(a) One-for-one checking (see 1.1(a)).

(b) Batch or control totals may be used to verify accuracy. However, since this procedure does not take into account items that negate each other, batch or control totals designed to verify completeness of input (see 1.1(b)) should also be used. These include:

- Dollar amount or quantity totals should be manually calculated for all input transactions within a batch prior to the input process. During input, these totals should also be calculated by the system and compared to the manual count.
- Hash totals are similar to dollar amount or quantity totals except that hash totals are generally performed on numeric fields that have no cumulative significance. For example, the sum total of the invoice dates appearing on each record represent a hash total.

(c) Computer matching (see 1.1(c)) may also be used to verify the accuracy of specific items; however, only those fields that exist in the masterfile can be subject to verification.

(d)   Programmed edit checks are designed to inspect various input fields and evaluate their amounts, formats, codes, and so on, for range or reasonableness. Fields may also be calculated and matched to other fields or files for their logical relationships. Required fields or items may also be flagged if they are left blank.

(e)   Prerecorded input entails preprinting various fields on forms or documents in order to ensure their accuracy. Examples of prerecorded input include optical or bar-coded product and/or serial numbers on inventory items, and magnetically coded account numbers on ATM or credit cards.

Authorization of Transactions

1.3   Controls over authorization of transactions are designed to ensure that only authorized or valid transactions are processed. All transactions should be subject to at least one of the following techniques in order to determine their validity:

(a)   Authorization by a responsible official should be required for all transaction data. This process may take place on-line (see (b)).

(b)   Security measures that restrict access to various administrative or accounting functions, terminals, programs and data should be employed (see 5.0).

(c)   Computer matching (see 1.1(c)) using masterfiles with preapproved standing/transaction data should be applied.

Handling of Rejected Transactions

1.4   All transactions rejected during editing (see 1.1, 1.2, and 1.3) should be identified, investigated, and corrected on a timely basis. Transactions should then be reintroduced to the system and subject to the same editing and control procedures as new (original) transactions. Procedures should be established to ensure that all rejected transactions are ultimately corrected and reprocessed. The following methods should be used to handle rejected transactions:
   •   When one or more transactions within a batch is rejected, the entire batch will also be rejected. No further processing of the batch will be allowed until corrections are made.
   •   Only rejected transactions will be removed from further processing. All transactions that pass the editing will be processed further. Any batch or control totals used must be adjusted appropriately.
   •   In both cases above, rejected transactions will be handled in either of two ways:

(a)   Rejected transactions will not be recorded in the system in any way. However, if the first method described is used, the rejected batch number should be recorded (see 1.1(d)).

(b)   Rejected transactions will be recorded in the system but will be segregated from accepted transactions by placing them in suspense files, awaiting corrective action.

Completeness and Accuracy of Computer-Generated Data/Transactions

1.5   Controls over computer-generated transactions are concerned that associated data is complete and accurate. (Examples of computer-generated transactions include automatic reordering of inventory and automatic posting of disbursements to the general ledger.) Controls should be established to ensure that data used in the generation of other data is complete, accurate, and authorized, and that associated parameters are input accurately as well. The following should be addressed:

- Key data used in the generation of transactions should be complete, accurate, and authorized (see 1.1 to 1.4).
- Programmed edit checks should be implemented to examine input parameters for reasonableness (see 1.2(d)).
- Programs that generate transactions should be logical, accurate, and secure (see 2.0 and 4.0).
- Results of processing (e.g., control totals) should be checked manually (see 1.2(b)).

Completeness and Accuracy of Updating

1.6   Update of data controls is needed to ensure that masterfiles are completely and accurately updated. Controls should be established to ensure that all transactions are updated accurately to relevant files once and only once.

- To ensure the completeness of update, at least one of the methods described in the completeness of input section (see 1.1) should be used.
- To ensure the accuracy of update, at least one of the methods described in the accuracy of input section (see 1.2), excluding the prerecorded input method, should be used.

2. SYSTEM/PROGRAM IMPLEMENTATION

Policy Management should apply controls over system and program implementation to ensure that appropriate procedures are applied to production programs when new systems become operational.

General A well-designed system requires careful planning and coordination between users and data processing personnel. A poorly planned system may result in lack of adequate controls and user satisfaction. There should be adequate involvement by users and data processing personnel during the key stages of design, testing, implementation, and final approval of new systems. Involvement between the user and programmers in developing specifications also ensures that appropriate control features are incorporated into the application. These controls include methods such as run-to-run balancing to ensure completeness and accuracy during processing.

Policies and procedures for the implementation of systems and programs are required so that data is complete and accurate. Depending on the size of the organization and the complexity of data processing, these standards should be communicated through a policies and procedures manual (see Documentation Index (Figure 2-1) for a list of items to be included). The procedures should define the duties and responsibilities of both user and data processing personnel.

Associated Materials Documentation Index (Figure 2-1, see page 19)

Procedures **Management of System Development**

2.1 All programming activities should be adequately planned and supervised. Tasks, responsibilities, and milestones should be clearly designated and documented. Progress should be tracked and monitored.

Periodic status meetings should be held, with any project changes documented and approved.

System Design

2.2 Controls should be in place to ensure that the design of the system/program is appropriate to the organizations' accounting and functional requirements. Specifications should be reviewed and approved by both user and data processing personnel. This applies to both modifications and specifications.

Vendor-Supplied Packages

2.3 Controls over the implementation of packaged (vendor-supplied) software should ensure that the system meets accounting and control requirements, as described throughout this manual. In addition to the implementation controls mentioned within this section, other vendor-related issues should be addressed as follows:

- Whenever possible, packages under consideration should be well recognized within the appropriate industry and should be in relatively common use.
- The vendor's contract should provide support throughout the package's expected life.
- To the extent possible, vendors should provide assurance that their packages have been adequately tested and quality assured.

System and Programming Standards

2.4 Programming standards should be applied to ensure that new systems interact correctly with the existing systems and contain adequate control features. To determine the interaction and effect of new applications, joint user and data processing effort is required to develop new application specifications. The involvement of a technical support group ensures that appropriate system software is selected for use with the new application. Typically, there are compromises between users and data processing to provide as many desired features as possible within the constraints of the available resources, both financial and personnel related.

Testing

2.5 Procedures should be in place to require that all new systems/programs be thoroughly tested before implementation.

- Test plans should be developed and include the scope and description of tests to be performed, the methodology for developing test data, and desired results.
- Both users and data processing personnel should approve test plans.

Testing procedures and test results should be checked by individuals outside of the programming group.

- New-system testing should extend from individual program testing to a system test in its entirety. Also, new systems should be tested with existing systems to ensure that they interface properly.
- A new program/system should be subjected to an adequate test period. Significant new systems can require parallel testing before final sign-off by users and data processing. As with modifications, the type of testing performed can vary but should always be independently reviewed and approved.

Cataloging

2.6　Cataloging is the method used to move new programs into the production environment (see 3.3).

Documentation

2.7　Guidelines should be established to ensure that documentation provides a complete understanding of the application system.

- Documentation should be prepared and maintained such that all individuals involved in an application system (users, programmers, operators, management, etc.) have sufficient information and instructions with which to perform their respective functions.
- System documentation should provide an overall description of the system including the system objectives, functions, original and updated system specifications, system interfaces and dependencies, hardware requirements, maintenance requirements (e.g., back-up, installation of new versions), control features (manual as well as computerized), and constraints.
- User documentation should provide detailed instructions on how to use the system properly. It should include various control procedures, such as those described in 1.0, as well as examples of all forms, input and menu screens, reports, and so on. User documentation should also address such issues as security, output routing and responsibilities.
- Program documentation should provide programmers with information necessary to revise and improve the existing system and to assist in the resolution of any processing problems as they occur. Program listings, detailed descriptions of program functions, and format layouts of input and output files should be included. Logic flowcharts and report layouts should also be illustrated.
- Operations documentation should provide the computer operator(s) with information necessary to run the system, including run instructions for processing various jobs and procedures for handling emergency situations (see 4.0). Run instructions should include job set-up

instructions, specification of parameters to be entered by the operators, restart and recovery procedures, and output requirements.

Standing Data Conversion

2.8   Controls should be established to ensure that during system conversion data is transferred completely and accurately, and that new data that is set up is complete, accurate, and valid. A conversion plan should be developed such that the results of the conversion process are data files that are complete, accurate, and valid. Standing data conversion controls should ensure that during system conversion standing data is transferred completely and accurately from the old system (including manual systems) and that no unauthorized changes are made to the data. The following issues should be addressed:

- Standing data fields should be identified.
- Application users as well as data processing personnel should be involved in the conversion process.
- Controls should be implemented to prevent the introduction of fraudulent or erroneous data to the standing data files (see 4.0).

Transaction Data Conversion

2.9   Transaction data conversion controls should ensure that during system conversion transaction data is transferred completely and accurately from the old system and that no unauthorized changes are made to the data. The following techniques should be employed:

- Batch or control totals (see 1.1(b) and 1.2(b)) should be used to determine the completeness and accuracy of the conversion.
- Record counts should be checked for completeness.
- Files should be balanced between the old and new systems.

Set-Up of New Data

2.10   Controls are needed to ensure that new data not found on, or converted from, the old system is completely and accurately created and recorded, and that it has been authorized. The following items should be addressed:

- Sources from which the new data will be obtained should be identified.
- Calculations needed for the development of new data should be identified.
- All input data used in the calculations mentioned above should be complete, accurate, and valid (see 1.0).
- Procedures for the appropriate approval of new data should exist.

Sample Documentation Index

System Documentation

    System narratives
    System overview flowcharts
    Source documents descriptions
    Output descriptions
        • reports
        • files
    File descriptions
    Special security provisions

Program Documentation

    Program narratives
    Program flowcharts (where applicable)
    Detail file layouts
    Data element descriptions
    Tables and table element descriptions
    Report layouts or samples
    Parameter listings and descriptions
    Source code listings
    Source code compilation listings
    Record of changes to programs

Operations Documentation

    Operations flowcharts, showing all input, all output, and program sequencing
    Program (job) operating instructions
        • set-up instructions
        • input files
        • input parameters
        • output files and reports
        • report distribution requirements
        • expected messages and responses
        • restart and recovery procedures
        • balancing procedures (where applicable)
    Data file retention requirements
    Contingency/emergency procedures

User Documentation

    System overview description
    System overview flowcharts
    Procedural sequencing presentation
    Source documents and descriptions
    Output descriptions
        • reports
        • files
    Functional organization chart
    Data input instructions
    Key controls descriptions and procedures

3. PROGRAM MAINTENANCE

Policy   Maintenance controls should ensure that changes to programmed procedures are designed appropriately and implemented effectively.

General   Controls over maintenance focus only on the process that should be followed for program modifications. These controls should include the handling of the request, programming, testing, the approval to move the program into the production environment, and the actual move to production.

Associated
Materials   Sample Service Request Form (Figure 3-1)
Sample Cataloging Authorization Form (Figure 3-2)

Procedures   **Internally Maintained Applications**

3.1   Internally maintained applications are programs that are enhanced, or supported, in house. Regardless of who makes the modification, there should be procedures that are followed consistently throughout the organization.

3.1.1   An organization can make use of contract programmers to enhance or maintain a system. These outside programmers should still follow the same development and testing procedures as in-house programmers (see 3.1.2 to 3.1.5). Also, all appropriate documentation should be properly updated before the contract with the programmers expires (see 2.7).

3.1.2   Completeness of changes should be ensured via a manual or computerized system to track change requests from submission to implementation. A service request form (Figure 3-1) or a memo to initiate the request should be required for all maintenance whereby management can establish that all requests have been considered and, if so, prioritized and implemented on a timely basis.

3.1.3 The user and data processing personnel should be involved in evaluating the reasonableness of the modification request and the acceptance of the modification. Both parties should meet to discuss costs/benefits and identify alternatives, if possible. Once validity of the request has been established, approval should be evidenced by the user and relevant data processing personnel.

3.1.4 A procedure should be established whereby management considers all major requests and decided actions to be taken, including setting priorities for outstanding requests.

3.1.5 Modifications should be properly tested and approved before being placed in production. The extent of the testing depends on the significance of the change. The following methods should be considered:

(a)   Unit testing occurs when the modified program alone is tested and not the programs with which it interfaces.

(b)   System or integrated testing occurs when a complete system or an integrated portion thereof undergoes testing regardless of where the modification was made.

Controls should be implemented to prevent production ("live") files from being used in testing.

Testing procedures should be designed to prevent unauthorized coding from being inserted into the program. This can be done either by source-to-source comparison or by using system software.

Regardless of the type of testing performed, an independent review and approval of test results should be made by the user.

3.1.6 Procedures should be established to ensure that all relevant system and/or program documentation is properly updated (see 2.7).

Vendor Maintained Packages

3.2   Controls over maintenance to package systems by their respective vendors should ensure the validity and proper implementation of modifications. Most of the procedures described in 3.1 should still apply.

3.2.1 Whether modifications are introduced by the vendor or user, approval by the user and appropriate data processing personnel as to the appropriateness of the modifications with regard to the user's requirements should be made.

3.2.2 Proper testing procedures should be followed regardless of who modifies the package (see 3.1.5).

3.2.3 The documentation described in 2.7 should be appropriately updated either by the vendor or user.

Cataloging

3.3 Cataloging is a method of moving amended programs into the production environment. The following procedures should be in place to ensure that only tested and approved programs are transferred from the test to the production environment.

3.3.1 Different versions of each program should be distinguishable so as to ensure that the most current versions of the programs are the ones subject to modification.

3.3.2 Controls should be established to ensure that unauthorized changes cannot be made to programs between the time they are tested and approved and the time they are transferred to production status. The use of an intermediate secured library should be considered for this purpose.

3.3.3 Only programs that have been properly approved and tested (see 3.1) should be transferred to production status. A cataloging authorization form (Figure 3-2) should be used to ensure and document that proper approval and testing has occurred. Care must be exercised to ensure that the versions of the programs involved in the transfer are the same versions that were in fact tested and approved.

3.3.4 All relevant program libraries (e.g., source, object, procedure) should be properly updated with the appropriate versions.

It would be preferable that the above procedures be executed by someone other than the programmer who developed and tested the program.

SECTION II
FIGURE 3-1

Sample Service Request Form

| PART I | (Completed by Requesting Department) |

Service Request Description _____
_____
_____
_____
_____

Expected Benefits _____
_____
_____
_____
_____

| PART II |

User Department: Requested by _____ Date _____

                    Approved by _____ Date _____

Data Processing: Approved by _____ Date _____

```
                          Data Processing Use Only
        SRF No. _____
        Estimated Effort _____
        SRF Disposition _____
                        _____
```

Sample Cataloging Authorization Form

| PART I | (Completed by Programmer) |

Program Name _____

Library Name _____

Modification Description _____

_____

_____

Target Implementation Date_____

| PART II | (Completed by Reviewer) |

Job Control Statements Reviewed _____

Documentation Updated and Reviewed _____

Operations Procedures Updated and Reviewed _____

Test Results Reviewed_____

| PART III |

User Department: Requested by _____ Date _____

                   Approved by _____ Date _____

Data Processing: Approved by _____ Date _____

Data Processing Use Only

Implemented (Date) _____

Signed _____

Company Name	Date
Approval	

4. *COMPUTER OPERATIONS*

Policy   Computer processing should be performed on a consistent basis.

General   Computer operations controls ensure that authorized programmed procedures are consistently applied, that correct data files are used, and that processing can be properly resumed in the event of system failures.

**Associated
Materials**   Sample Operations Schedule (Figure 4-1)

Sample Operator Incident Log (Figure 4-2)

Procedures   **Scheduling**

4.1   The primary control considerations in job scheduling are whether jobs are run at the appropriate points in time and in the correct sequence. When on-line application systems are in operation, scheduling will be relevant only to regular batch jobs, end-of-day or period routines, and back-up and housekeeping routines.

4.1.1   Daily operations schedules (Figure 4-1) for all jobs and programs to be run should be prepared and approved by a responsible individual.

4.1.2   Controls should be established to ensure that all jobs and programs are processed in accordance with the schedules. Any departures from the schedules should be documented and approved by a responsible individual.

Job Set-Up and Execution

4.2   Operators should be provided with written procedures and instructions regarding the set-up and execution of each application job or program (see 2.7.4). These instructions should be developed and approved by responsible representatives from the computer operations and application user groups.

4.2.1 Controls should be established to prevent or detect unauthorized changes to approved job set-up instructions, including processing parameters. Any variations to job set-up instructions should be documented and approved by a responsible individual.

4.2.2 Parameters and options are used in setting up and operating system software. Effective control over system software normally includes the review and approval of its set-up and operation procedures by a responsible individual.

Use of Correct Data Files

4.3 Controls should be established to ensure that the correct data files are used during processing. Such controls require that each file be uniquely identified. Common methods used to implement these controls include software-generated internal file labels, generation data groups, and the use of an automated tape management system. In addition, where applicable, these controls should ensure that all volumes of a multivolume file are used. Any departures from these procedures should be documented and approved by a responsible individual.

Operator Actions

4.4 Control procedures should cover the actions of computer operators, such as supervision and review of their work. In on-line systems, data files normally are available to users at all times, so that relatively little operator intervention is required. In batch systems, each job is set up separately and files may need to be loaded by operators. Thus, computer operations controls may be of greater concern.

4.4.1 Controls should be established to ensure the proper identification and reporting of all abnormal conditions: system failures, system restart or recovery, emergency situations, and so on.

4.4.2 Adequate supervision of operators should be provided at all times, including shifts outside normal working hours. Supervision should include regular reviews of operator actions. Particular attention should be given to situations described in 4.4.1 to ensure that processing results were not adversely affected.

Activity Logs

4.5 In most computer systems, the logging of system activities is a feature of system software—usually the operating system. (Controls over the implementation, maintenance, set-up, and execution of system software were discussed in 2.0, 3.0, and 4.2.2.) Depending on the amount of activity and the types of activities recorded, system logs can become too voluminous to be printed and reviewed in a practical manner. In such circumstances, logs are used only to review and investigate system failures, operator actions, or other unusual occurrences (Figure 4-2).

4.5.1 In order to rely upon activity logs for supervision and review of operations, controls should be established over the completeness and accuracy of those logs. Common methods include the use of sequentially prenumbered pages that are physically controlled, accounted for, and show the start and stop times for the period covered.

4.5.2 Normally, system software will prevent anyone from making modifications to logs or the method of logging. Any changes made to system logs or to the method of logging should be documented and approved by a responsible individual.

Back-Up and Recovery

4.6 Controls over recovery from processing failures require that data be regularly copied as back-up, that the processing status at the time of failure can be established, and that procedures ensure that proper recovery takes place. Involvement by the various user groups will help ensure that recovery takes place properly.

(a) Controls should be established to ensure that copies of all data files are backed up at appropriate intervals, based on the normal business cycle (i.e., how often data on the files change).

(b) Controls should be established to ensure that program libraries are regularly backed up, together with a record of changes made between back-ups.

(c) Controls should be established to ensure that data files and programs are recovered properly after a processing failure and that errors are not introduced during the recovery process. Should modifications to data files or programs be necessary during an emergency situation, procedures should ensure that all changes made are accurate and authorized.

(d) To ensure that back-up copies of data files and programs are available for recovery during an emergency situation, back-up media should be stored in an off-site facility. Preferably, the off-site location is secure and environmentally protected as well as sufficiently remote to realistically serve its purpose.

(e)   A contingency plan should be developed that ensures the continuity of applications processing in the event of an unexpected interruption of computer services, taking into account and documenting possible risk scenarios. Once a plan has been developed, approved, and documented, it should be periodically tested in order to ensure that all its pieces work properly and remain consistent.

SECTION II
FIGURE 4-1

Sample Operations Schedule

Date_____   Day _____

Daily Jobs	(1)	(2)	Weekly Jobs	(1)	(2)	Periodic Jobs	(1)	(2)
_____	—	—	_____	—	—	_____	—	—
_____	—	—	_____	—	—	_____	—	—
_____	—	—	_____	—	—	_____	—	—
_____	—	—	_____	—	—	_____	—	—
_____	—	—	_____	—	—	_____	—	—
_____	—	—	_____	—	—	_____	—	—
_____	—	—	_____	—	—	_____	—	—
_____	—	—	_____	—	—	_____	—	—
_____	—	—	_____	—	—	_____	—	—
_____	—	—	_____	—	—	_____	—	—
_____	—	—	_____	—	—	_____	—	—
_____	—	—	_____	—	—	_____	—	—
_____	—	—	_____	—	—	_____	—	—
_____	—	—	_____	—	—	_____	—	—
_____	—	—	_____	—	—	_____	—	—
_____	—	—	_____	—	—	_____	—	—
_____	—	—	_____	—	—	_____	—	—
_____	—	—	_____	—	—	_____	—	—
_____	—	—	_____	—	—	_____	—	—
_____	—	—	_____	—	—	_____	—	—
_____	—	—	_____	—	—	_____	—	—
_____	—	—	_____	—	—	_____	—	—
_____	—	—	_____	—	—	_____	—	—
_____	—	—	_____	—	—	_____	—	—
_____	—	—	_____	—	—	_____	—	—

(1) Check off when job is completed.

(2) Note any error/amend codes. Refer to incident log for disposition.

SECTION II
FIGURE 4-2

Sample Operator Incident Log

Date	Time	Description of Trouble	Disposition/Explanation
____	____	_____	_____
____	____	_____	_____
____	____	_____	_____
____	____	_____	_____
____	____	_____	_____
____	____	_____	_____
____	____	_____	_____
____	____	_____	_____
____	____	_____	_____
____	____	_____	_____

Company Name	Date
Approval	

5. *SECURITY*

Policy   Access to information stored on a computer should be restricted.

General   Management should identify and classify computerized resources (data, programs, hardware, etc.) and protect them with a well-organized combination of software and manual procedures. Security software provides the ability to restrict access to the system at various levels: system, application, application function, data file, and data element. Adequate security features may be available in the operating system, specialized access security software, or within individual application packages. The latter is usually not as desirable in that it is not always applicable to the entire data processing environment.

Associated Materials   Sample Access Request Form (Figure 5-1)

Procedures   **Overall System Access Controls**

5.1   Controls should be established to prevent unauthorized access to the system and to restrict each user's access based on specific job-related functions. The operating systems for many mid-range computers provide the facilities to accomplish these restrictions. For example, based on a user's ID and password (see 5.3) the operating system will force the user into a restricted workshell/menu out of which the user cannot venture. All unauthorized attempts to bypass access controls should be reported and promptly investigated.

Security Policy

5.2   Management should develop and communicate a security policy stating their position on information security. Such a policy should consist of a set of written guidelines promoting rules and criteria about the treatment of computerized resources.

Security Administration

5.3 Administration of access security controls should be performed by responsible individuals independent of the programming function.

(a)   Only duly authorized individuals should be assigned system IDs and passwords that permit access to the system. An access request form (Figure 5-1) should be used to ensure and document proper authorization. Each ID should be unique in order to track user activities and provide for accountability.

(b)   Passwords should be used to ensure the correct identification of authorized users by the system. Passwords should be kept secret, not easily guessed, and changed on a regular basis.

(c)   All access privileges should be promptly canceled or amended for terminated or transferred employees.

(d)   Adequate security and controls should exist over the ability to perform administration of all of the functions mentioned above (e.g., maintenance of security tables, changing of passwords, granting special privileges).

(e)   Periodic security reviews should be conducted to ensure that access privileges granted remain appropriate.

Dial-Up Access

5.4 Controls should be established to prevent unauthorized access via dial-up mechanisms. Public access can be restricted through the use of automatic dial-back procedures, among others.

Physical Access

5.5 Physical access to all computer facilities and other areas identified as containing sensitive information should be limited at all times, including evenings, weekends, and holidays. Computer facilities include terminals, modems, and communications lines, as well as the computer itself. Depending on the circumstances, physical access should be treated with the same formalities as described in 5.2 for system access (e.g., authorization required, use of special badges or keys).

Custody of Data and Programs Stored Off-Line

5.6 Magnetic tapes, diskettes, and removable disks containing programs or data files, including back-up copies, should be protected and uniquely identified.

5.6.1 Control procedures should be established over the existence and movements of all off-line media. Numbering on external labels should be used to account for all media movements. Such movements usually include issuance from and return to the computer room, media library, and off-site storage facility.

5.6.2 Off-line media should be stored in secure environments and should be accessible only by individuals authorized by management.

Utilities and High-Level Programming Languages

5.7 The use of high-level programming languages and utility programs that can be used to modify data files should be restricted to appropriate personnel authorized by management. In addition, the use of such programs should be closely monitored by a responsible official for appropriateness.

Bypassing Normal Access Controls

5.8 When it becomes necessary to bypass normal access security controls, such as during emergency situations, the action should be authorized by a responsible official. Such authorization may be informal at the outset of the conditions that caused the temporary change in policy, but formal written authorization should nevertheless be provided after the fact. It is also important to ensure that normal access security controls are reinstated as soon as possible and that any changes to data files have been properly controlled and approved.

Output

5.9 Data security extends beyond the physical domain of computer hardware.

5.9.1 Often overlooked as a potential security exposure, printed reports containing sensitive information should be produced only according to an approved schedule (see 4.1) or when requested with the authorization of a responsible official.

5.9.2 Sensitive output that is not printed directly but is held on-line or transmitted to a remote computer should be controlled to prevent or detect changes to the output prior to printing and to ensure that the output reaches only its intended destination.

SECTION II
FIGURE 5-1

Sample Access Request Form

| PART I | (Completed by Requesting Department) |

Name _____ Tel Extension_____

Department_____ Location _____

Functional Description _____

Specify Access Required _____
_____
_____
_____

If other user in department has identical access needs, give name_____

| PART II |

User Department: Approved by _____ Date _____

Data Processing: Approved by _____ Date _____

> ### Data Processing Use Only
>
> Entered by _____ Date _____
>
> Verified _____
>
> Menu Name _____

Section III

GENERAL LEDGER AND JOURNAL ENTRIES

Company Name	Date
Approval	

1. *MAINTAINING AN EFFECTIVE ACCOUNTING SYSTEM*

Policy   The company should establish and maintain an effective accounting system to capture data regarding the economic activity of the enterprise.

General   Management requires accurate and timely financial reports in order to judge the performance of the enterprise and plan for future activities.

Associated Materials   None

Procedures   **General Ledger Set-Up and Posting**

1.1   The company should set up a general ledger system to quickly and accurately accumulate all financial transactions. The framework for this system is called the chart of accounts. The chart of accounts consists of the account titles and account numbers assigned to the titles. The account titles should be developed from an understanding of the economic activity and the information management deems necessary in the financial reports. Account titles should most appropriately describe the assets, liabilities, owner's equity, revenues, and expenses of the company.

The following account titles in the chart of accounts are representative of what might appear in a simple business enterprise:

Assets:
    Cash
    Accounts receivable
    Allowance for doubtful accounts
    Inventory
    Prepaid expenses
    Land

> Building
> Equipment
> Furniture and fixtures
> Accumulated depreciation
> Other assets

Liabilities:
> Accounts payable
> Accrued expenses
> Payroll taxes payable
> Notes payable

Owner's Equity:
> Capital stock
> Retained earnings

Revenue:
> Sales
> Miscellaneous revenue

Expenses:
> Cost of goods sold
> Wages
> Payroll taxes
> Insurance
> Rent
> Repairs and maintenance
> Utilities
> Depreciation expense
> Interest expense
> Income taxes

Arrangement of Account Titles

1.2   Account titles within the chart of accounts should generally be arranged in the following order:

- Assets
- Liabilities
- Owner's Equity
- Revenue
- Expenses

1.2.1   Within these categories, current accounts are grouped first, followed by long-term accounts. Referring to the sample chart of accounts shown in 1.1, note that current assets such as cash, accounts receivable, and inventory are listed before long-term assets such as land and building.

1.2.2   After the accounts are titled and listed in order, account numbers should be assigned. Generally, accounts should be numbered in the following manner:

1000–1999	Assets
2000–2999	Liabilities
3000–3999	Owner's Equity
4000–4999	Revenue
5000–end	Expenses

1.2.3 Expenses are often divided into several groupings. For instance, a manufacturing enterprise may use the following grouping:

5000–5999	Cost of goods sold
6000–6999	Billing expenses
7000–7999	General and administrative expenses

Establishment of Contra Accounts

1.3 Accounting systems record transactions at their historical cost. However, there are instances where generally accepted accounting principles require that an account be presented in the financial reports at a lesser amount. This is accomplished through the use of contra accounts, allowing the accounting system to maintain records of the accounts at historical cost while reducing their value for financial reporting purposes. For example, accounts receivable is stated at its historical cost. However, for financial reporting purposes, accounts receivable must be reduced for accounts that will not be collected. Therefore, the allowance for doubtful accounts is established to reduce accounts receivable to its collectible amount.

Financial Information Adequacy

1.4 Accounting systems should provide adequate financial information on a divisional or subsidiary level if deemed necessary.

Although business enterprises are extremely concerned with their overall operating results, they often require more detailed information to know how various segments of the business are performing. Businesses with more than one profit center, division, or subsidiary must know detailed information about each area to determine if it is profitable or not.

Different methods can be used to accomplish these accounting needs depending on the requirements of the enterprise. If an organization will use centralized accounting for all of its profit centers, divisions, and subsidiaries, adding additional numbers to the standard chart of accounts will serve to accumulate the required information. For example, a retail sales organization with three stores could use the following system:

4000–001	Sales—Store #1
4000–002	Sales—Store #2
4000–003	Sales—Store #3

Adding these additional codes to all accounts in the chart of accounts will give the organization all of the detail it will require for each store. Most computerized accounting systems will be able to use the 001, 002, and 003 codes to produce financial reports for each store, as well as a combined report to show the overall financial position and results of operations of the organization.

In larger organizations, different divisions and subsidiaries may require their own separate accounting system. The main consideration in this circumstance is to arrange the charts of accounts for each entity so that they are consistent with each other. They should be arranged consistently so that the operating results of each division or subsidiary can be quickly merged with the operating results of other divisions or subsidiaries to produce the overall results for the entire organization.

2. GENERAL LEDGER ACTIVITY

Policy   All valid general ledger entries, and only those entries, should be accurately recorded in the general ledger.

General   The general ledger consists of control accounts for accounts in the enterprise's chart of accounts (see 1.0). These accounts are listed in the general ledger in numerical order with the account title. The general ledger may be maintained on a computer in a bound book of ledger pages, or on loose ledger cards.

Associated Materials   Journal voucher (Figure 2-1)

Procedures   **Posting Monthly Activity to the General Ledger**

2.1   At least monthly all activity should be posted to the general ledger. The postings to the general ledger accounts may come from any and all of the following sources:
- General journal—adjusting journal entries
- Sales journal—sales and accounts receivable activities
- Purchases journal—expense and accounts payable entries
- Payroll journal—payroll summary
- Cash receipts journal
- Cash disbursements journal

The physical posting of the general ledger will vary depending on the type of system being used. Most computer accounting software packages are fully interactive and post journal activity to the general ledger on command by the computer operator. Manual systems require the summarization of journal activity and then carrying the totals forward to the general ledger. The posting to the general ledger should be referenced as to its source. For example, the December 31 entry from page 101 of the sales journal might be referenced as follows:

12/31	SJ101	10,000

After posting to the general ledger, the control accounts should be retotaled to reflect the new balances. The general ledger accounts should then be re-added to determine that the general ledger is in balance after the posting from journals.

Documentation of Entries Not Originating from Journals

2.2 All entries (recurring and nonrecurring) that do not originate from journals should be supported by journal vouchers (Figure 2-1) that are prenumbered.

Accounting systems record transactions as they occur on a historical cost basis. However, simply recording transactions as they occur does not always provide an accurate basis for reporting the financial position and operating results of an enterprise. For instance, an enterprise may purchase a piece of equipment and pay cash for it. However, the equipment must be depreciated over its useful life rather than expensed when purchased. Likewise, other adjustments are periodically required to adjust the recorded transactions, such as accruing certain items of income and expense or correcting posting errors.

2.2.1 Certain entries, called recurring adjusting journal entries, are made every period. These entries include, but are not limited to, the following:

- Depreciation of fixed assets
- Amortization of intangible assets
- Amortization of prepaid expenses
- Amortization of deferred revenue
- Accrual of interest expense on notes that are not paid within each accounting period

The company should identify these recurring adjusting journal entries for posting to the general ledger in each accounting period. Most computerized accounting systems allow the company to set up recurring adjusting journal entries, and these entries are posted to the general ledger automatically as part of the closing process.

2.2.2 Nonrecurring adjusting journal entries must be prepared to properly reflect account balances. Nonrecurring adjusting journal entries include, but are not limited to, the following items:

- Correction of posting errors
- Accrual of income and expense items
- Recording of noncash transactions

Adequate Documentation for All Journal Vouchers

2.3 All journal vouchers for journal entries should be prepared only on the basis of adequate supporting documentation.

Authorization of Entries

2.4 All journal vouchers for entries into the general ledger should be authorized by a responsible official who is not involved in the origination of the entries.

Review of All Authorized Vouchers

2.5 A review should be performed of the sequential voucher numbers to ensure that all entries have been made.

SECTION III
FIGURE 2-1

Journal Voucher

_____ Company   Date _____

Number _____

Account Name	Account Code	Debit	Account Name	Account Code	Credit

Explanation:

_____

Prepared by _____   Date _____

Approved by _____   Date _____

3. *ADEQUATE GENERAL LEDGER MAINTENANCE*

Policy   The general ledger should be adequately maintained.

General   As stated throughout this section, the general ledger accounts are the source of all of the financial reports used by management. It is therefore critical that the accounting records, after the entry of transactions in them, are properly controlled so that they continue to reflect accurately the operations of the business.

Associated Materials   None

Procedures   **Preparation of Trial Balance**

3.1   A trial balance should be prepared periodically (preferably monthly) from the general ledger. A trial balance is a listing of all general ledger accounts and their balances as of a particular date. The trial balance will verify that the general ledger accounts balance (debits equal credits) and serves as a workpaper to make adjustments to any accounts to correct their balances.

Performance of Reconciliations

3.2   Reconciliations should be performed between control accounts maintained in the general ledger and the subsidiary ledgers.

Review of Trial Balance and Reconciliations

3.3   The trial balance and the reconciliations should be reviewed by a responsible official (by persons other than those who post entries in the general ledger). The reasons for differences noted should be investigated and any adjustments properly processed.

Close of Income and Expense Items

3.4   At the end of the fiscal year, all items of income and expense should be closed so that they will not carry over to the next fiscal year. After all of the required adjustments have been made to the general ledger, the company should prepare a closing entry. A closing entry is an entry that will create a zero balance in each revenue and expense account when the entry is posted to the general ledger. Since these accounts will not balance, the entry will include a credit to retained earnings of the enterprise for the net income, or a debit to retained earnings for the net loss of the enterprise. After the closing entry is posted to the general ledger, the income and expense accounts should be zero, and the general ledger is ready to begin accepting transactions for the next fiscal year.

Section IV

CASH

1. *CASH MANAGEMENT*

Policy   The company should maintain an effective system of cash management that anticipates cash needs and plans adequately to satisfy them.

General   Cash is required to pay for all assets and services purchased by the company and to meet future obligations as they come due. The disbursement of cash, therefore, is a regular occurrence, and a sufficient level of cash should be kept available to meet these requirements. However, cash is not a productive asset as it earns no return. Therefore, only cash necessary to meet anticipated day-to-day expenditures plus a reasonable cushion for emergencies should be kept available. Any excess cash should be invested in liquid income-producing instruments.

Associated
Materials   Short-Term Investment Vehicles (Figure 1-1)
Three-Way Budget (Appendix D)

Procedures   **Maximizing Return on Idle Funds**

1.1   Cash not required for operations should be invested. The more common types of temporary investments are described in the chart on short-term investment vehicles (Figure 1-1). (See also Section VIII—1.0.)

Expediting of Cash Receipts

1.2   The time lag between goods shipment or service performance and the deposit of funds to the company's bank account should be kept to a minimum.

(a)   Invoices should be issued at the time of shipment or service performance.

(b)   All customer remittances should be sent to a single address unless multiple location lockboxes are utilized (see 1.2(d)).

(c)   Consideration should be given to offering early payment discount terms (i.e., 2/10 net/30) in order to promote quicker customer payment.

(d)   Consideration should be given to having all customer remittances sent directly to a bank lockbox. Banks will provide a daily list of receipts and many will allow borrowing based upon the average balance of remittances in the lockbox account in what is called a zero-balance account.

Collection Practices

1.3   A review of accounts receivable listings for past due balances should be performed on a continuous basis. Delinquent accounts should be contacted immediately, not after the next billing cycle. See Section V—1.0 for more detail on collection procedures.

Deferring Disbursements

1.4   Cash disbursements should be released at the latest acceptable time, without affecting relationships with vendors. Early payment discounts should be taken advantage of if they result in benefit. Checks should be mailed at the end of the day and, if possible, at the end of the week.

Cash Budgets

1.5   A cash budget should be prepared in order to effectively manage cash balances. The budget should be built around the three basic aspects of cash management: operations, cash flow, and financial condition (See Appendix D—the "three-way budget"). It is reprinted by permission of John Wiley & Sons, Inc.

The budget should be prepared on an annual basis, broken down by month. Monthly reports will let you monitor each component by comparing actual performance with budget, both for the current month and cumulatively.

SECTION IV
FIGURE 1-1

Short-Term Investment Vehicles

Type of Investment*	Usual Maturity	Minimum Investment	Liquidity	Interest Paid	Description
Money market funds	7 days average	$ 1,000	Marketable	Daily	Mutual funds concept of diversified investments with portfolio management
Certificates of deposit	30 days–1 year	100,000	Marketable	At maturity	Bank time instrument issued for a specified period earning interest at a stated rate
Bankers' acceptances	30–270 days	10,000	Marketable	At maturity	Time draft drawn on and guaranteed by a bank
Repurchase agreements	1–29 days	25,000	———	At maturity	Sale of securities with agreement to repurchase at maturity at a stated price and rate
Commercial paper	5–270 days 30–270 days 90–270 days	100,000 50,000 25,000	Nonmarketable	At maturity	Unsecured promissory note issued by a corporation to meet short-term cash needs
U.S. Treasury bills	To 1 year	10,000	Marketable	At maturity	Short-term U.S. government obligation

*Due to rapid changes in investment vehicles, check with your investment advisor for the most up-to-date information.

Reprinted by permission of John Wiley & Sons, Inc.

2. *CASH RECEIPTS*

Policy　Control should be established over all cash and checks received, and they should be deposited promptly in the company's bank accounts.

General　Cash receipts should be protected from misappropriation. Physical access to cash receipts and cash receipt records should be limited to authorized personnel. Additionally, cash receipts should be recorded in the appropriate period.

Associated Materials　None

Procedures　**Opening the Mail**

2.1　The mail is to be opened and a listing of cash and/or checks received should be prepared under the supervision of a responsible official.

(a)　The individuals preparing the list of cash receipts (typically the cashier) should be persons other than those who deal with:
- accounts receivable,
- accounts payable, or
- the general ledger.

(b)　The listing of cash receipts should include the name, amount, discount taken, invoice number, date, and the total of all receipts.

(c)　When a lockbox is used, the bank should provide the company with a list or computer file of the cash receipt information.

Endorsement of Checks

2.2　In situations where cash receipts are received directly by the company, checks should be restrictively endorsed immediately.

Bank Deposits

2.3   All cash sales and check remittances should be deposited intact daily.

Reconciliation of Cash/Checks Received to Bank Deposit

2.4   Records of cash receipts and summaries should be compared to deposit slips and bank statements by persons other than those who handle cash receipts (e.g., as part of the bank reconciliation procedure in 5.0).

Summarize Cash Receipts

2.5   Records of cash receipts should be summarized and totals established for posting to the cash receipts journal.

3. DISBURSEMENTS FROM BANK ACCOUNTS

Policy Disbursements from bank accounts should be made only for valid transactions.

General The payment for goods and services, whether accomplished by check or bank transfer, should be organized to ensure that no unauthorized payments are made, that complete and accurate records are made of each payment, and that payments are recorded in the appropriate period. Additionally, physical access to cash and unissued checks must be restricted to authorized personnel.

Associated Materials Check Request Form (Figure 3-1)
Check Control Log (Figure 3-2)

Procedures **Preparing Checks and Bank Transfers**

3.1 Checks and bank transfers should be prepared based on the determination that the transaction is valid and is in accordance with the following company procedures:

3.1.1 A determination that the transaction is valid should be accomplished by reviewing the following supporting documentation as applicable:
- Invoices (together with receiving reports and purchase orders)
- Payroll records
- Petty cash vouchers
- Remittance advices
- Check requisitions (see Figure 3-1)

All supporting documentation should be signed by a responsible official indicating proper authorization.

3.1.2 Checks and bank transfers should be prepared by persons other than those who initiate or approve any documents that give rise to disbursements.

3.1.3 Checks and bank transfers should be designed or completed in such a way to make subsequent unauthorized alteration difficult through the use of protective paper, check imprint, and so on.

3.1.4 The following procedures should be prohibited:
- Checks payable to "bearer" or "cash"
- Checks signed in blank
- Altered checks and bank transfers

Check Signing

3.2 Checks should be signed by officials ("signatories") other than those who approved the transaction for payment. Depending on the size of the company, this official may be the president, a vice-president or the controller.

3.2.1 Each signatory should examine the original supporting documentation to ensure that each item has been checked and approved in accordance with the company's procedures.

3.2.2 There should be adequate control over the custody and use of the signer and signature plates if a mechanical check signer is used.

3.2.3 Consideration should be given to establishing a dollar level whereby two signatures will be required for disbursements in excess of such dollar level.

Three-copy checks should be used, with two of the copies having "nonnegotiable" printed on them. The copies of the checks should be distributed as follows:
- Vendor (negotiable copy)
- Attached to voucher package
- File of numerical sequenced check copies (this file may not be necessary if the company has a detailed check register)

Disbursement of Checks

3.3 After signing, all checks should be forwarded directly to the payee (or to the bank with the bank transfer authorization) without being returned to the originators or others who are in a position to introduce documents into the cash disbursement system.

Cancel Supporting Documents

3.4 The supporting documents should be canceled by the signatory (or under the control of the signatory) to prevent subsequent reuse.

Maintenance of Check Control Log

3.5 A separate record of checks being processed should be maintained by using a control log (Figure 3-2). The control log should contain:
- the sequence of checks issued;
- the name of the person to whom the checks are issued;
- the date the issue was made;
- the signature of the custodian in charge of the supply of unissued checks;
- if applicable, the sequence of checks returned and/or voided; and
- the signature of the person who has returned voided or unused checks.

3.5.1 All checks should be sequentially prenumbered so that it can be established that all checks have been accounted for.

Ideally, all transactions should be recorded on prenumbered documents. Although they can be sequenced after preparation, the first method is preferred. In many systems where the computer generates checks, the check will contain two numbers, the preprinted number and the number printed by the computer. These two should be the same (in some systems they are not) to make control easier.

3.5.2 The usage of checks should be accounted for by reconciling the quantity of checks issued to cash disbursement records. This should be performed by persons other than those who have custody of unissued checks.

3.5.3 Supplies of unissued checks should be properly safeguarded.

Summarize Cash Disbursements

3.6 All checks and bank transfers should be summarized and recorded in the appropriate books of original entry. (This summary reflects the credit to cash and debit to accounts payable. See Section X for summarizing invoices/accounts payable.)

SECTION IV
FIGURE 3-1

Check Request Form

CHECK REQUEST	No. 501

TO: ACCOUNTING DEPARTMENT

Please issue check payable to:

Name _____   Date _____

Street _____   Amount $ _____

City _____

Purpose _____
_____
_____

Charge to _____

Instructions: Mail to Payee _____

                  Deliver to _____   _____
                                                            Authorized Signature

SECTION IV
FIGURE 3-2

Check Control Log

Date	Checks Issued	Issued to	Approved	Returned	Voided	Returned	Approved

4. *IMPREST AND SIMILAR FUNDS*

Policy Reimbursement of imprest and similar funds (e.g., used for payment of payrolls, postage, and branch office expenses) should be made only for valid transactions.

General Imprest accounts are usually limited to a nominal balance, and deposits are in amounts equal to the totals of checks drawn (or to be drawn) on the accounts.

Associated Materials None

Procedures **Disbursement of Funds**

4.1 Prior to the disbursement of any funds, a voucher should be prepared with supporting evidence such as payroll records, receipts, or other miscellaneous supporting detail and approved where appropriate. See 3.0 for more detail on cash disbursement procedures.

Summarize Disbursements

4.2 A summary of all disbursements should be maintained (e.g., petty cash book) and an analysis should be performed in order to charge the proper general ledger accounts.

Reimbursement of Imprest Funds

4.3 Periodically, the imprest account should be replenished so as to bring the balance up to the imprest amount. The amount replenished should equal the sum of all imprest account disbursements since the previous reimbursement and any differences should be reconciled.

Payment of Payroll Through Imprest Funds

4.4 Imprest funds are often used for payment of payrolls. In this case, a deposit is made to bring the balance up to a desired amount and disbursements are made subsequently (rather than replenishing the balance as in 4.3). A reconciliation should be performed between the imprest amount and the payroll journal and any difference should be reconciled.

Post Activity to the General Ledger

4.5 Based upon the summary generated in 4.2, a journal entry should be prepared, approved, and posted to the general ledger.

5. *BANK RECONCILIATIONS*

Policy   Adequate steps should be taken to confirm the accuracy of the bank balances shown in the general ledger.

General   Generally monthly, data on cash receipts and disbursements journals should be compared with the details reported on bank statements. Unmatched and mismatched data are used to reconcile the book and bank balances. The reconciliations may be performed manually by general accounting personnel (who do not have access to cash and are not involved in processing or recording cash transactions), or they may be performed by the computer when the organization's cash records are computerized and banks furnish statements on computer-readable media.

Associated Materials   Bank Reconciliation (Figure 5-1)

Procedures   **Preparing Bank Reconciliations**

5.1   Bank balances, as shown by the bank statements, should be reconciled regularly with the general ledger balance. Data on cash receipts journals and cash disbursement journals should be compared on an item-by-item basis with the details reported on bank statements. Mismatches should be listed for investigation.

   The person who prepares the reconciliation (Figure 5-1) should receive the bank statements directly from the bank and retain them until the reconciliations are completed.

Determination of Reconciling Items

5.2   Discrepancies between general ledger cash balances and closing balances reported on bank statements usually result from transactions recorded in cash journals but not yet processed and recorded by banks (such as deposits in transit and outstanding checks) and items on bank statements not yet processed and recorded by the company (such as bank service charges). Most of those items do not require investigation.

Generally, accounting personnel (who do not have access to cash and are not involved in processing and recording cash transactions) should investigate all significant:

- unmatched data in cash receipts and disbursements journals that fail to clear banks within a reasonable period of time,
- unmatched items on bank statements unanticipated or judged erroneous by the company, and
- mismatched items in cash receipts and disbursements journals and bank statement items.

Review of Bank Reconciliation

5.3   Bank reconciliations and proposed adjustments to general ledger cash balances and cash detail files should be reviewed and approved by general accounting and finance management.

Bank Reconciliation

Month_____

A/C # _____

Balance per Bank $

Less Outstanding Checks

Add Deposits in Transit

Other Adjustments

Balance per General Ledger $ _____

_____

Prepared by   Date

_____

Reviewed by   Date

Section V

REVENUE CYCLE

Company Name	Date
Approval	

1. *CREDIT POLICIES*

Policy Determination of an appropriate credit policy should be made by management personnel.

General Establishing credit terms and discounts is a business decision which includes determining the credit to be extended, the type and amount of discounts, the length of the discount period, return and adjustment policies, and special financing arrangements.

There are four primary discounts:

- Trade discounts—discounts off list prices, particularly related to volume levels.
- Discounts for prompt payment—allows customers to take a discount if they pay within a set period of time after billing.
- Cash discounts—allows customers to pay a lesser amount for a cash purchase than they would if they bought on credit.
- Employee discounts—allows employees to take a discount off list prices.

Determining customer credit limits is an economic and business process requiring judgment of which credit policy best serves the company's total interests. It should be recognized that increasing the length of the credit period increases the cost of holding receivables and the period the company is at collection risk.

Associated Materials None

Procedures **Segregation of Duties**

1.1 Credit department personnel should not perform any accounts receivable or cash receipts functions.

Customer Credit Check

1.2 The credit department should request information on the customer's financial resources and debts and check with credit bureaus. On the basis of this information, the credit department should determine, in accordance with company policy, whether to sell on credit to that customer.

Establishment of Credit Guidelines

1.3   Guidelines (credit scoring methods) should be created and credit limits should be established for all customers.

Credit Limit Increases

1.4   Credit limits should be increased only upon review of the customer's payment history and written approval of appropriate personnel.

Accounts Receivable Agings

1.5   Accounts receivable agings should be reviewed periodically to identify overdue accounts and potential collectibility problems.

1.5.1   Based on previously established written guidelines, consideration should be given to suspending credit to customers with overdue accounts.

1.5.2   Continued sales to such customers should be on a COD basis only.

Security Interest in Items Sold

1.6   If deemed appropriate to obtain a security interest in the items sold, filings for such interest should be timely.

Guidelines for Collection of Delinquent Accounts

1.7   Written guidelines should be established for determining the timing of various steps and methods to be used, including the institution of formal collection procedures, against delinquent accounts.

2. CUSTOMER PURCHASE ORDERS

Policy An orderly system should be established for processing and monitoring customer purchase orders for products or services.

General A customer generally prepares a purchase order, which provides authorization for the company to provide a product or service. Confirmation of the order and a controlled system of processing the request can prevent customer dissatisfaction and loss of revenue due to inaccurate or lost sales orders.

Associated Materials Sales Order Form (Figure 2-1)
Shipping Log (Figure 2-2)

Procedures **Customer Purchase Order Log**

2.1 Customer purchase orders, both verbal and written, should be logged in a sales order book when received.

Prenumbered Sales Order Forms

2.2 Prenumbered sales order forms (Figure 2-1) should be completed for all customer orders (both written and oral). The form should have the appropriate number of copies to enable it to be used to advise the related departments of the requisite actions (i.e., credit approval, requisitioning, packing, shipping, and invoicing).

(a) The sales order form should be compared with the customer's purchase order for accuracy and completeness.

(b) If confirmation of the order is desired, a copy of the sales order form may be sent to the customer. When order processing time is very short, a telephone call may be more practical. The call should be documented, including name and title of customer personnel, date, and disposition.

(c)   Copies of the sales orders should be maintained in a holding file in numerical sequence until the order is complete, then the form is matched with the corresponding invoice.

(d)   The file should be reviewed periodically and incomplete sales orders should be investigated. In addition, the file can be used to assist management in determining the order backlog.

(e)   When a partially completed invoice is used in lieu of a sales order form, a copy should be maintained in a holding file until shipment and completion of the invoice. The file should be reviewed for incomplete sales orders as above.

Credit Department Approvals

2.3   Approval for credit by the credit department should be obtained on a timely basis and documented in writing before orders are processed.

Sales Order Form as Requisition for Merchandise

2.4   A copy of the sales order form or partially completed invoice may be used to requisition goods from finished goods inventory.

(a)   Goods should not be released without proper authorization.

(b)   The items should be physically counted by an employee who is not the custodian of finished goods and such count documented on the sales order forms or partially complete invoice.

Sales Order Form as Packing Slip

2.5   A copy of the sales order form or partially completed invoice may be used as a packing slip. Shipping documents may also include a shipping label on which the name and address of the shipper, the customer, and the destination are indicated, and a bill of lading.

(a)   Before packing the order, the forms should be examined for all appropriate authorizations (e.g., credit approval).

(b)   The requisitioned items should be compared to the documents to ensure that the correct goods and quantities are being prepared for shipment.

Shipping Log Preparation

2.6   A shipping log (Figure 2-2) should be maintained and reviewed periodically to ensure that all sales are properly recorded.

Sales Order Form

_____ COMPANY
SALES ORDER

SALES ORDER NO.	CUSTOMER ORDER NO.	CUSTOMER DATE	PAGE OF	SALES ORDER DATE

	C H A R G E T O			TERMS
				F.O.B.

REQUIRED ROUTING		Collect	Prepaid	CUSTOMER NO.

PRODUCT CODE	ITEM NO.	Original Qty. Ordered	PART NUMBER	DESCRIPTION	SHIPPING SCHEDULE	UNIT PRICE

	SPECIAL INSTRUCTIONS AND MARKS	
		SALES TAX %
	PACKAGING REQUIREMENTS ☐ COMMERCIAL ☐ OTHER	APPROVAL

ORDER BILLING MASTER

SECTION V
FIGURE 2-2

Shipping Log

_____ COMPANY

Customer	Shipping Information	Sales Order Number	Shipping Date

3. *REVENUE RECOGNITION*

Policy   All sales should be recorded accurately and on a timely basis.

General   The preparation of a sales invoice generally initiates the formal recording of revenue. Control over invoicing is established by authorization to bill and is based upon supporting documents such as the customer's order, sales order form, shipping order, and evidence of shipment.

**Associated
Materials**   Sales Invoice (Figure 3-1)

Procedures   **Prenumbered Invoices**

   3.1   Prenumbered invoices (Figure 3-1) should be prepared or completed for all goods shipped or services performed.

Invoicing Procedures

   3.2   Invoicing procedures should include the following:
   - Customer names should be compared with a master customer list or customer orders.
   - Quantities should be based on actual records of products shipped or services performed and compared with sales orders. Differences (other than back orders) should be investigated.
   - Prices should be based on established price lists or approved sales orders. Pricing exceptions (changes) should be approved by an appropriate individual.
   - Invoice extensions and additions should be recomputed by an individual other than the preparer of the invoice.
   - All invoices should be recorded in the sales journal.

Sales Journal Review

   3.3   The sales journal should be reviewed periodically for numerical sequencing. All missing invoice numbers should be investigated.

Sales Journal Summarization

3.4   The sales journal should be summarized and reviewed for mathematical accuracy.

Sales Journal Posting to General Ledger

3.5   The posting of the sales journal summarization to the general ledger control account should be reviewed and approved by a responsible official.

Review of Shipping Log or Service Records

3.6   The shipping log or service records should be reviewed periodically to identify goods shipped or services performed that have not been invoiced.

SECTION V
FIGURE 3-1

Sales Invoice Form

_____ **COMPANY**

SALES INVOICE

SALES ORDER NO.	CUSTOMER ORDER NO.	CUSTOMER DATE	PAGE OF	SALES ORDER DATE	INVOICE NUMBER	INVOICE DATE

CHARGE TO

			TERMS		SHIPMENT DATE	
			F.O.B.		SHIPPED VIA	
					WAYBILL NUMBER	
					NO. OF PACKAGES	WEIGHT

REQUIRED ROUTING

Collect	Prepaid	CUSTOMER NO.	SHIPMENT NUMBER	Partial	Complete	TERMS CODE

PRODUCT CODE	ITEM NO.	Original Qty. Ordered	PART NUMBER	DESCRIPTION	SHIPPING SCHEDULE	UNIT PRICE	QUANTITY ON BALANCE	QUANTITY THIS SHIPMENT

SPECIAL INSTRUCTIONS AND MARKS

Work Order #

	TOTAL
SALES TAX	%	SALES TAX
	FREIGHT

PACKAGING REQUIREMENTS	COMMERCIAL OTHER	APPROVAL	PAY THIS AMOUNT ➤➤	TOTAL AMOUNT

4. ACCOUNTS RECEIVABLE

Policy   Accounts receivable records should be accurate, complete, and maintained in a manner to indicate the length of time the customers' debt has been outstanding.

General   Accounts receivable arise from sales on credit to customers. The account is relieved by the posting of receipts from the cash receipts journal, approved credit memos for allowances, or returned merchandise and write-offs of uncollectible accounts.

Associated Materials   None

Procedures   **Posting Sales Invoices**

4.1   Posting of sales invoices to the accounts receivable subsidiary ledger should be performed by individuals independent of cash functions.

Posting as an Independent Function

4.2   The general ledger control account should be posted by individuals independent of the accounts receivable and cash receipts functions.

Timely Identification of Errors

4.3   Consideration should be given to mailing monthly statements to customers to allow for timely identification of errors in addition to prompting collections.

Posting of Adjustments

4.4   Payments, partial payments, credits, and other authorized adjustments to accounts receivable should be posted against the corresponding invoices in order to maintain the accurate aging of the accounts receivable subsidiary ledger.

Reconciliation of Accounts Receivable Subsidiary Ledger

4.5 The accounts receivable subsidiary ledger should be reconciled to the general ledger control account monthly. All differences should be investigated and resolved. The reconciliation should be reviewed by a responsible official.

Review of Credit Balances

4.6 A review of credit balances should be performed periodically by reviewing the accounts receivable subsidiary ledgers or the accounts receivable aging.

Review of Cutoffs

4.7 Files of unmatched shipping reports and unprocessed invoices, the sales journal, the cash receipts book, and other relevant records should be reviewed to determine that all activity has been recorded in the appropriate accounting period.

5. CUSTOMER RETURNS AND ALLOWANCES

Policy Returns and allowances should be controlled, documented, and recorded.

General The return of goods by the customer results in adjusting receivables and inventory. Allowances are less frequent yet difficult to ascertain. They are often based upon evaluations of customers' complaints.

Associated Materials Credit Memorandum (Figure 5-1)

Procedures **Written Authorization**

5.1 Written authorization should be given to customers to permit (authorize) the return of goods when appropriate.

Count and Examination of Returned Goods

5.2 Authorized returned goods should be counted and examined in the receiving department and a receiving report prepared. The condition of the goods should be noted on the report.

Issuance of Credit Memo

5.3 The return authorization should be compared to the receiving report and approved, and a prenumbered credit memo prepared. Credit memos should contain all important information to support the appropriate journal entry and for posting to the accounts receivable subsidiary ledger. Returns and claims should be recorded in the accounts as quickly as possible in order to maintain the correct balances of revenues and accounts receivable.

Separate Check of Mathematical Accuracy

5.4   The mathematical accuracy of the memos should be reviewed by someone other than the preparer.

Authorization of and Conditions for Allowances

5.5   The conditions under which allowances may be given and the personnel authorized to do so should be documented in writing.

Approved Allowances

5.6   Approved allowances should be documented on a prenumbered credit memo.

Review of Credit Memo Numerical Sequence

5.7   The numerical sequence of the credit memos should be reviewed periodically. All missing numbers should be investigated and accounted for.

Valid But Unprocessed Claims

5.8   The open file of unmatched receiving reports should be reviewed periodically to identify valid but unprocessed claims.

SECTION V
FIGURE 5-1

Credit Memorandum

No. 12345

VENDOR NO. _____

DATE _____

P.O. NO. _____

CHARGE _____

ATTN: ACCOUNTS PAYABLE

REF. INV. NO. _____

ITEM	DESCRIPTION	PART NO.	QUANTITY	UNIT PRICE	AMOUNT

Authorized Signature   Date

6. *OTHER REVENUES*

Policy Other types of revenue should be recorded on a timely basis.

General Revenues flow into a company from sources other than the conventional sale of products and services. Rent and royalties are examples of the more common sources.

Associated Materials None

Procedures **Rental Income**

6.1 • Lease agreements should be reviewed and a schedule of rents to be received prepared.
• Rental receipts should be noted on the schedule.
• The schedule should be reviewed on a timely basis and appropriate action taken for delinquent accounts.
• Prepayments should be recorded as unearned revenue until the designated time has elapsed.

Royalties

6.2 • Agreements should be reviewed and a schedule of receipts should be prepared.
• Royalties received should be noted on the schedule.
• If the royalties are not a fixed amount, the calculations and extensions should be reviewed for mathematical accuracy and adherence to the agreement.

Deferred Income

6.3 Deferred income relates to revenue for which the service has not been performed or the goods have not been delivered (i.e., service contracts, magazine subscriptions, etc.).

- Schedules should be prepared indicating the appropriate points in time at which the revenue is to be earned and recorded.
- The schedules and corresponding journal entries should be reviewed and approved by a responsible official.

Barter Transactions

6.4   Barter transactions should be recorded at the estimated fair value of the goods or services received, and the barter revenue should be recognized when it is earned.

Section VI

PRODUCTION CYCLE

Company Name	Date
Approval	

1. *SALES AND PRODUCT FORECASTS*

Policy Management should establish policies concerning forecasting, appropriate production plans and rates, capacity, usage, and on-hand inventory levels.

General The forecasting of future sales of products and the usage of components/raw materials is critical in production planning and control.

"Top-down" forecasting starts with general business conditions. A forecaster/budgeter then translates that information, given specific industry and company attributes, into the sales the company anticipates.

"Bottom-up" forecasting starts with the individual product sales expectations, formulated by input from salesmen, customers, and other forecasters. Both methods should be employed and compared to arrive at a reasonable budget for sales.

Other factors to be considered include the plant's optimal operating capacity and the hiring of extra employees or lay-offs in seasonal periods.

Associated Materials None

Procedures **Preparation of Sales Forecasts**

1.1 A sales forecast for the year broken down by month or other useful period should be prepared and approved by appropriate levels of management.

Determination of Production Volume

1.2 Based upon the approved forecast, determination of specific volumes of production should be documented in a production plan approved by appropriate levels of management.

- Machine and labor hours should be scheduled as called for by the production plan.
- Raw materials levels should be assessed to ensure that sufficient quantities will be available to meet the production schedule.

Review of Production Levels and Related Sales

1.3 Actual production levels and related sales should be reviewed frequently to allow for timely cost-effective adjustments to production scheduling. Such adjustment should be approved by appropriate levels of management.

```
┌─────────────────────────────────────────────────────────────────┐
│                                                                   │
│  ─────────────────────────────────      ─────────────────────    │
│  Company Name                            Date                     │
│                                                                   │
│  ─────────────────────────────────                               │
│  Approval                                                         │
└─────────────────────────────────────────────────────────────────┘
```

2. COST-FLOW METHODS

Policy   Determination of a cost-flow assumption and method of allocating production costs should be made by appropriate levels of management.

General   Various cost-flow assumptions may be used including specific identification; first in, first out (FIFO); last in, first out (LIFO); and variations thereof. Within FIFO and LIFO, the most common conventions utilized are average cost and standard cost.

Direct labor and material may be charged via a standard cost system or specific job orders. Other production costs (indirect costs) should be allocated by either of the following methods:

- Direct costing—Variable indirect costs (e.g., indirect labor) are allocated to units produced, and fixed indirect costs (e.g., factory rent) are accounted for as a period expense. If this method is used, the company needs to have the ability to convert to full absorption for external reporting.
- Full absorption costing: All variable and fixed indirect costs are allocated to all product units produced.

Finished goods are normally accounted for on the same basis as raw materials (FIFO, LIFO, etc.) and include accumulations of various raw materials, component parts, and production costs.

Associated Materials   None

Procedures   **Determination of Appropriate Method**

2.1   Determination of the most appropriate cost method should be made by appropriate management levels.

Consistent Use of Method Selected

2.2   The methodology selected should be utilized consistently.

Allocation of Production Costs—Overhead Application Rate

2.3 Once management has established a policy of allocating production costs, an overhead application rate should be determined and applied. Methods of application might include:

- machine-hours,
- direct labor dollars,
- direct labor hours.

Proration of Variance and Under/Over Absorbed Overhead

2.4 Price and quantity variances as well as under/over absorbed overhead may occur and should be prorated among inventories (work in progress and finished goods) and cost of goods sold for the period as appropriate.

Variance Analysis

2.5 Upon identification, variances should be analyzed by appropriate personnel to allow for corrective action, when feasible, to be taken on a timely basis.

Review of Standard Costs and Overhead Rates

2.6 Standard costs and overhead rates should be reviewed periodically by appropriate personnel and revised as necessary.

Company Name	Date
Approval	

3. *INVENTORY CONTROL*

Policy   Procedures to provide physical security for all inventory (raw materials, component parts, work in progress, finished goods, and other) should be established.

General   Cost/benefit analyses should be utilized to ascertain the optimum level of security that should be provided (e.g., locked storage areas, site security guards, etc.). Relative value, likelihood of theft, and ease of removal/loss are factors to be considered in drawing a conclusion.

Associated Materials   Materials Requisition Form (Figure 3-1)

Procedures   **Custodial Control of Operations**

3.1   A responsible custodian should have control of the operations.

Written Procedures for Inventory Custody

3.2   Specific written procedures over the custody of inventory items between initial receipt and recording into the inventory records should be established.

Authorization for Movement of Inventory

3.3   Authorization for all movement to and from each storage/work area should be in writing.

(a)   Prenumbered material/component part requisitions (Figure 3-1) should be prepared in triplicate by the department/area needing the items, with proper written authorization indicated on the requisition. The requesting department should keep a copy of the requisition and send the other two copies to the inventory department.

- Upon receipt of the requisition, inventory personnel should issue the requested items to the applicable department, retaining a copy of the requisition for posting to the perpetual inventory and sending the last copy to accounting for posting to the general ledger inventory accounts.
- Numerical sequence of the requisitions should be reviewed for completeness periodically, with proper follow-up on missing requisitions.

(b) Work-in-progress inventory is usually more difficult to account for than raw materials or finished goods as it may be scattered throughout the production facilities, in various stages of completion, or in the hands of outside processors at off-site locations.

- Procedures recording transfers to and from work in progress should be established. (Note: Movement of inventory between departments during the production process should be reported for operational purposes but often is not recorded for accounting purposes.)
- When appropriate, documentation of the related raw materials component parts (and direct labor) should remain with work in progress.
- A log documenting shipments and subsequent returns should be maintained of all work in progress sent for outside processing. The log should be reviewed for any items outstanding for more than the normal turnaround time.
- Guidelines should be established as to when defective work in progress becomes designated as spoiled or scrap. Authorization for such adjustments should be in writing.

(c) Movement of finished goods should be controlled.

- Movement of inventory into finished goods should be controlled by numerical sequence of receiving reports or by reconciling inventory additions to production reports.
- Finished goods should be released for shipment only upon the receipt of authorized sale and shipping documents.
- Returns of finished goods should be authorized, documented, and appropriately recorded.

Independent Check of Transferred Items

3.4   Items should be counted and recorded at the time of transfer by others than those who have custody of the inventory.

Reconciliation of Regularly Scheduled Physical Counts

3.5   Physical counts of quantities of inventory should be scheduled on a regular basis. The counts should be reconciled to the inventory records and general ledger (see 5 and 7).

SECTION VI
FIGURE 3-1

Materials Requisition Form

UNIT NO. _____ Company Requisition _____ JOB NO. _____ DATE _____

PAGE _____ OF _____

C O D E	PART NUMBER	PART DESCRIPTION	QUANTITY				UNIT COST	TOTAL COST
			REQ'D	ISSUED	RETURNED	B/O		

ISSUED BY	RECEIVED BY	DATE ISSUED	TOTAL =
APPROVED BY			

Company Name	Date
Approval	

4. *PERPETUAL INVENTORY*

Policy Management should determine whether or not to utilize and maintain a perpetual inventory.

General Many companies do not use a perpetual inventory system for various reasons:

- Small size of the inventory
- All production is for custom orders
- Small number of company personnel
- Slow turnover of inventory
- Lack of sophistication in accounting records

Use and maintenance of a perpetual inventory is the preferred method; without it, management is unable to determine costs incurred for production of inventory, volume, and the dollar value of inventory on hand at any one moment.

Associated Materials None

Procedures **Perpetual Inventory Not Used**

4.1 If a perpetual inventory is not maintained, all costs incurred are charged to purchases or cost of sales.

Opening Inventory Balance

4.2 When the physical inventory is counted, costed out, and summarized, the opening inventory balance is "trued up" with a corresponding adjustment to cost of sales.

5. *PERIODIC PHYSICAL INVENTORY*

Policy A physical count of all inventories should be made periodically (at least annually).

General Physical counts of all types of inventory may be taken concurrently at one time or periodically (cycle counts) throughout the year.

Associated Materials Inventory Tag Example (Figure 5-1)

Procedures **Proper Control of Physical Inventory**

5.1 The physical inventory should be properly supervised and controlled.

Concurrent Physical Inventories

5.2 When all inventories are physically counted concurrently, a greater effort is required of each of the participating departments of accounting, production, and warehousing/inventory control because a larger volume of counting is necessitated.

5.2.1 Operations should be suspended or significantly reduced.

5.2.2 Instructions to company personnel concerning the physical inventory should be written and include:

- location, date, and beginning time of physical inventory;
- number and composition of count teams;
- designated inventory "area" of each count team and second count team assignment;
- detailed directions on how to fill out inventory tags or sheets (lbs., gal., pallets, colors, boxes, bags, manufacturer, etc.) in order to expedite the subsequent reconciliation process;

- identification of damaged or obsolete inventory and scrap;
- description of stage-of-completion for work in process;
- identification of inventory held for others;
- control of the inventory tags or sheets (Figure 5-1) issued and used;
- accumulation of appropriate cut-off information.

5.2.3 Inventory should be maintained in an orderly arrangement to facilitate the count.

5.2.4 Inventory should be properly identified and described, including stage of completion when appropriate.

5.2.5 Counters should be aware of the possibility of obsolete and slow-moving items, as well as inventory with a deteriorating value or of questionable quality (excessive dust, presence of rust, scrap, goods rejected by quality-control department), in accordance with the written instructions for the physical inventory. These items should be noted on the inventory tags or sheets and brought to the attention of the count supervisor for follow-up.

5.2.6 The count and second team recount should be reconciled and all differences resolved.

5.2.7 All sheets or tags used during the physical count should be accumulated and accounted for before the count teams leave the area.

5.2.8 See 7.0 for reconciliation of the physical inventory to the perpetual inventory.

Frequent Period Physical Counts

5.3 Periodic counts should cover all inventory items at least once during the year but may be more frequent for active or fast-turning inventory items.

5.3.1 Physical inventories taken periodically throughout the year require:
- perpetual records that are up to date;
- functioning internal controls;
- controls over physical movement (e.g., purchases, finished goods released into inventory, and sales).

5.3.2 Fewer people are required for the actual counting on periodic inventories as a smaller portion of the inventory is being counted at one time, and a shutdown of operations is not usually required.

5.3.3 Counters should be aware of inventory with deteriorating value or of questionable quality. These items should be noted and brought to the attention of the count supervisor for follow-up.

5.3.4 Management should perform unscheduled test counts on occasion to maintain the accuracy and integrity of the inventory.

Inventory Not on Premises

5.4 Inventories not on the premises include items out on consignment or for subcontract work, items in railroad cars, shipments to a customer site that are rejected, or any other situation for which the inventory is recorded on the books but is not in the company's physical control.

5.4.1 Detailed records of such inventory should be maintained.

5.4.2 The records should be reviewed periodically by appropriate personnel.

Inventory Held in Public Warehouses

5.5 Theoretically, inventories held in public warehouses do not need to be physically counted, as the warehouse should maintain control of the items under its auspices and perform inventory counts on its own. If a decision is made to perform a physical count of inventories held by a public warehouse, the procedures are similar to those described in this section.

5.5.1 Arrangements should be made with management of the public warehouse for such a physical count.

5.5.2 The count should be compared and reconciled to the internal records of the warehouse.

5.5.3 The count should be reconciled to the records of the company, with resolution of any differences/discrepancies.

Proper Identification of Inventory Ownership

5.6 All inventories belonging to others should be clearly identified and physically segregated to avoid any erroneous inclusion in the company's inventory counts.

5.6.1 If the amount is significant and the activity frequent, perpetual records should be maintained.

5.6.2 This type of inventory should also be counted during the physical inventory but excluded from the inventory valuation.

Indirect Materials and Supplies Inventory

5.7   Materials and supplies are items that are required to be on hand or are a part of the production process, for example, small hand tools, replacement parts for machinery, catalysts in a chemical process, cleaning fluids.

(a)   Preferably, a perpetual inventory should be maintained with a physical inventory taken at least annually, and comparisons made and discrepancies investigated.

(b)   Depending on the size of the inventory, management may elect to expense the items as they are purchased or to capitalize them and charge to expense as they are used.

Reconciliation of Physical to Perpetual Inventory

5.8   The actual physical inventory quantities counted should be reconciled with the amounts per the perpetual inventory.

(a)   Specific items to be taken into account are inventories on the perpetual listing but not found in the physical inventory (reconciling items):
- Items sold and shipped, but not removed from the perpetual
- Items added to perpetual through purchases, but not yet received
- Items physically unaccounted for through error, theft, and so on
- Items scrapped but not removed from the perpetual

Inventories counted in the physical inventory but not on the perpetual listing (reconciling items):

- Items sold and removed from perpetual but not physically segregated and excluded from the physical inventory
- Items physically added to inventory through purchases or completion of work in process, but not reflected on the perpetual
- Items held on consignment
    Although not a part of the physical inventory, items in public warehouses or not on the premises should also be compared to the perpetual inventory and any necessary changes to the perpetual identified.

(b)   Once the perpetual inventory quantities have been adjusted to reflect the physical counts and other reconciling items, the corresponding extensions and footings should be adjusted.

(c)   Costing for items identified as slow moving, obsolete, or of questionable value should be adjusted accordingly to reflect the expected realizable value.

(d)   Any reconciling inventory item that appears unusual should be investigated.

(e)   Through the aforementioned reconciliation process, all identified changes to the perpetual inventory balances should be made and approved by an individual independent of the custody of or accounting for inventories.

SECTION VI
FIGURE 5-1

Inventory Tag Example

Tag # _____

Location: Area _____
        Row _____
        Column _____

Type: RM _____
      FG _____
      WIP _____

Qty _____

Unit of Measure _____ (gal., lb., bars, pallet, bag, tank, car, etc.) _____

Description _____

Inventory Coding_____ (batch #, lot #, etc.) _____

Remarks _____

Counted by _____
Checked by _____

6. *INVENTORY OBSOLESCENCE*

Policy   Management should establish a policy for evaluating inventory, material, component parts, and finished goods for obsolescence.

General   In addition to comparing the carrying cost of inventory with its market value, a comparison must also be made of the quantity of product on hand with the demand for it.

Associated Materials   None

Procedures   **Revalue Certain Inventory to Net Realizable Value**

6.1   If inventory on hand exceeds demand or there has been no activity in the past year nor any forecasted requirements, the obsolete or excess portion of the inventory should be reduced to an amount not less than its net realizable value. The difference should be charged to the current period expenses.

Disposal of Obsolete or Excess Inventories

6.2   Consideration should be given to disposing of the obsolete or excess inventory or offering it at substantially reduced prices in order to obtain a tax deduction for the write-off and generate cash flow.

7. *PERPETUAL INVENTORY*

Policy The general ledger should accurately reflect the perpetual inventory.

General In practice and in theory, the perpetual inventory should be the subsidiary ledger for the general ledger account. However, there may be reconciling items, including:
- allowance for obsolete, slow-moving items, if not taken into account at the individual item level;
- adjustment for lower of cost or market;
- adjustment for actual physical count.

Associated Materials None

Procedures **Adjustments to the General Ledger**

7.1 Adjustments to the general ledger account should be made to reflect actual physical counts.

Physical Count Summary Reviewed for Accuracy

7.2 The summarization of the physical counts should be reviewed for mathematical accuracy, including pricing, before adjustments are posted.

Approval for Posting to General Ledger

7.3 The posting of all inventory transactions and adjustments should be reviewed and approved by the appropriate personnel.

Section VII

PREPAID EXPENSES

1. MONITORING AND ACCOUNTING FOR PREPAID EXPENSES

Policy   The company should establish a method to monitor and account for prepaid expenses.

General   Prepaid expenses arise whenever cash is disbursed and a portion of the associated benefit of the disbursement is for a future period. An illustration of a prepaid expense is an insurance premium that is paid in a lump sum when the policy is issued or renewed and the policy covers multiple accounting periods. Consequently, an asset (prepaid expense) is recorded on the books for the total premium when paid and is charged (amortized) to expense ratably over the coverage period.

Associated Materials   Asset Register (Figure 1-1)

Procedures   **Reviewing Incoming Invoices to Ensure Prepayment**

1.1   The accounts payable department in conjunction with the accounting department should review the coding of incoming invoices to ensure that all prepayments are identified. A "tickler" file that lists large recurring payments by due date should be established as a reminder of upcoming payments.

Maintenance of Asset Register

1.2   Once identified, each expense should be maintained in an asset register (Figure 1-1) to better monitor the various types of prepaid expenses. The register should list the general ledger account number and title as well as a description of each asset, including vendor/supplier, type of service or coverage, benefit period, amount paid, expense for the period, and any other relevant information.

Amortization Periods and Rates

1.3   Once an expense has been entered in the asset register, the amortization period should be determined. For example, if an insurance invoice, billed quarterly, is paid at the beginning of the quarter, one-third should be charged to expense each month.

Some prepaid expenses may be amortized on a basis other than time. For example, brochures may be amortized as they are used (e.g., if 10,000 brochures are purchased and 6,000 remain at the end of an accounting period, it would be appropriate to have 60 percent of the cost set up as an asset as long as the value is retained).

Preparation of Standard Journal Entries

1.4   The accounting clerk should prepare a standard journal entry to record the monthly expense (established in 1.3) to ensure proper matching. The entry should be reviewed and approved by the accounting supervisor.

SECTION VII
FIGURE 1-1

Asset Register

Insurance _____ Account No. 335-1

Policy	Description	Company	Period	Date Paid	Amount Paid	Monthly Expense	Coinsurance
08461	Property & casualty	O.K. Ins. Co.	1/1/90–12/31/90		$12,000	$1,000	10%
94820	Bonding, fidelity	No. 1 Ins. Co.	2/6/90–2/6/92		9,000	375	None
46215	Boiler & machinery	Mutual Ins. Co.	1/1/92–12/31/92		6,000	500	None

Rent _____ Account No. 335-2

Description	Company	Period	Annual Amount Paid	Date Paid	Monthly Expense
Accounting office	A.C. Green	1/1/90–12/31/90	$60,000	12/18/90	$5,000
Plant #1	Rental Agency	1/1/90–12/31/92	48,000	12/31/92	4,000
Plant #2	Deal Associates	1/1/90–12/31/91	24,000	1/10/91	2,000

2. *CONTROLLING ASSET BALANCES*

Policy   Detailed records of prepaid expenses should be reconciled periodically with the control account.

General   Reconciliations should be performed to help ensure the accuracy of the detailed records and the control account.

Associated Materials   None

Procedures   **Preparation of Reconciliations**

    2.1   On a periodic basis, a reconciliation should be performed between the asset register and the general ledger balance. The person performing the reconciliation should not be one of the individuals who maintains the detailed records and the control account.

    Investigation of All Discrepancies

    2.2   All discrepancies should be investigated on a timely basis.

    Supervisory Review of the Reconciliation

    2.3   The reconciliation should be reviewed and approved by a responsible official such as the accounting manager.

Section VIII

INVESTMENTS

1. *INVESTMENT OF IDLE FUNDS*

Policy   Funds not presently needed for company operations should be invested. Such investments should be properly authorized and accurately accounted for.

General   The company should invest available funds in order to maximize earnings and minimize risk during the period of availability of the funds. The overall investment policy, specifying the needed liquidity of investments, acceptable risk, and expected returns, should be established by management and approved by the company's board of directors. The following is a description of certain types of investments a company might have. This listing is not intended to be all-inclusive but rather to present common forms of investments (see Section IV—1.1):

- Demand deposit accounts—offered by financial institutions. Include passbook savings, statement savings, and money market savings accounts.
- Time deposit accounts—also offered by financial institutions. Require that the deposit remain at the institution for a specified period of time. Withdrawal of the deposit prior to the expiration of that time period may result in a loss of earnings. A certificate of deposit (CD) is an example of a time deposit account.
- Bankers acceptances—short-term corporate notes payable. These notes are generally issued by the finance subsidiary of a corporation and are sold at a discount from face value with the discount representing earnings on the note during the period held by the purchaser.
- U.S. government obligations—include Treasury notes and bills issued by the U.S. government. Treasury notes bear interest at a specified rate payable semiannually. Treasury bills are sold at a discount from face value with the discount representing earnings during the period held by the purchaser.
- Municipal bonds—include tax-exempt, long-term debt issued by state and local government agencies. These bonds pay a specified interest rate over the life of the bond and may be sold at a premium over or a discount from face value.
- Corporate bonds—include long-term debt issues of corporations.

These bonds pay interest at specified rates and may be sold at either a premium over or discount from face value.

- Corporate stocks—include both common and preferred stock issued by public companies (those subject to the Securities and Exchange Acts of 1933 and 1934). The company may also have other common and preferred stock or partnership investments in closely held companies and affiliates (see Section 4.0).

Associated Materials

Investment Control Log (Figure 1-1 A and B)
Investment Purchase/Sale Authorization Form (Figure 1-2)
Investment Gain/Loss Calculation Worksheet (Figure 1-3)

Procedures **Investment Policy**

1.1 The board of directors should set the investment policy for the company. The investment policy should provide general guidelines regarding the type of investments deemed appropriate and the objectives of each investment (e.g., overnight deposits for excess cash, ninety-day Treasury notes for excess working capital, etc.). Management, specifically the treasurer or other officer, should be designated to implement the Board's investment policy. A specific set of procedures should be adopted to address the following areas, at a minimum:

- Designation of personnel to approve certain transactions such as purchases and sales
- Designation of personnel to have access to investment certificates
- Investment and investment earnings recording
- Designation of personnel to review and approve investment accounting, bank and broker statement reconciliations, adjustments to the carrying value of investments, and other decisions regarding investments.

Authorization of Investment Vehicles

1.2 Annually, the company's board of directors should authorize the use of specific depository and investment banks and brokerage firms. This authorization should be documented in the minutes of the applicable board meeting and communicated to the appropriate treasury and management personnel. Management should then communicate the authorization and a list of those personnel designated as authorized agents for the company to the appropriate banks and firms. As a part of the annual authorization process, management should evaluate the company's prior relationship with banks and brokerage firms to determine suitability for renewal. Such evaluation should consider service responsiveness, types of investments offered, quality of investment advice, service and transaction charges, and any other relevant criteria.

Authorization of Investments

1.3   All transactions regarding investments should be properly authorized by a designated official and recorded in an investment control log (Figure 1-1). Such transactions include:
- purchases;
- sales;
- movement to and from safekeeping (the physical safeguarding of assets through use of a vault, safe deposit box, or independent custodian [see Chapter 2].

Investment Purchases

1.4   Investment purchases should be made by check or bank transfer (see Section IV—3.1) after compliance with the following procedures:

(a)   A determination that the purchase transaction is properly authorized in accordance with company policy (see 1.1).

(b)   A determination that the investment authorization is properly documented by use of an investment purchase/sale authorization (Figure 1-1) or other form.

(c)   Preparation of a check requisition or a bank transfer request to accompany the investment purchase/sale authorization form.

(d)   Assignment of an investment number for authorization and control purposes. Investment numbers should be controlled and sequentially issued.

Investment Sales

1.5   Investment sales should be transacted after compliance with the following procedures:

(a)   A determination that the sale transaction is properly authorized (see 1.4(a)).

(b)   A determination that the authorization is properly documented by use of an investment purchase/sale authorization or other form.

(c)   The investment certificate should be sent to the agent handling the sale transaction for investments held on the premises (once (a) and (b) have been completed). Authorization to the agent should be communicated in writing. If investments are kept off site, authorization to release the document from safekeeping should be provided to the custodian. The custodian should provide the company with a receipt documenting the release from safekeeping. The receipt should be filed in the investment file (see 2.7).

(d)   The investment control log should be updated. An adjustment of the carrying value of the investment must be made to reflect partial or complete sale of the investment.

Investment Sales Gain or Loss

1.6   The expected gain or loss upon sale or other disposition of an investment should be calculated before a decision regarding the sale is finalized. The calculation should be updated/finalized subsequent to the sale. The gain or loss calculation should be documented in a prescribed format through the use of a standard form such as the investment gain/loss calculation worksheet (Figure 1-3). This form should be filed in the investment file.

Investment Sales Proceeds

1.7   Proceeds from the sale of investments should be received either by check or bank transfer. The check or bank transfer should be processed in accordance with the procedures outlined in Section IV—2.0. A copy of the receipt or deposit ticket should be included in the investment file.

Investment Results Reports

1.8   Monthly reports detailing the earnings and activity in all investment accounts should be prepared and distributed to appropriate management and board personnel.
The summary of all transactions should be recorded in the general ledger through the use of a journal entry. Journal entries should be reviewed by a responsible official.

Reconciliation of Investment Accounts

1.9   Investment account balances should be reconciled regularly with the general ledger balance. Such reconciliation should be reviewed and approved by a responsible official.

Investment Account Balances Agreed to Bank/Broker Statements

1.10   Amounts recorded on the supporting schedules should be reconciled to broker/bank statements at least quarterly and preferably monthly, if possible. For those investments held on the company's premises or at a safe deposit vault, quarterly physical inventories should be performed and reconciled to the supporting schedules. An authorized official should review and initial these reconciliations.

SECTION VIII
FIGURE 1-1A

XYZ Company
Investment Control Log

Purchases

Investment Number	Description	Authorization Date	Amount	Broker/ Agent	Trade Date	Settlement Date

SECTION VIII
FIGURE 1-1B

XYZ Company
Investment Control Log

Sales

Investment Number	Description	Authorization Date	Amount	Broker/ Agent	Trade Date	Settlement Date

Number _____

XYZ Company
Investment Purchase/Sale Authorization Form

Date _____   Investment Number _____

Investment Type _____

Investment Description _____

Amount: Purchase _____

          Sale _____

Expected Trade Date _____

Expected Settlement Date _____

Broker/Agent _____

Commission _____

Other Expenses _____

Safekeeping Arrangements _____

_____

_____

_____

	Signature	Title	Date
Preparer	_____	_____	_____
Authorization	_____	_____	_____

Three copies of this form should be prepared, with distribution as follows:

    original—investment file
    copy #1—attached to check request
    copy #2—retained by preparer
    copy #3—numerical sequence file maintained with the investment control log

SECTION VIII
FIGURE 1-3

XYZ Company
Investment Gain/Loss Calculation Worksheet

Date _____ Investment Number _____

Investment Type   _____
       Description   _____

Original Purchase Price _____

Premium (subtract) or
  Discount (add)
  Amortization   _____

Amortized Cost at / / _____

Less Valuation Allowance _____

Net Carrying Value   _____ A

Gross Sales Proceeds   _____

Less Selling Expenses   _____

Net Proceeds   _____ B

Gain or (Loss) (B – A)   ===============

Comments

_____
_____
_____

	Signature	Title	Date
Preparer	_____	_____	_____
Authorization	_____	_____	_____

2. *SAFEGUARDING OF INVESTMENTS*

Policy   All investments should be safeguarded against physical loss or misuse.

General   All investments should be properly controlled to safeguard against theft, misuse, or damage. Certificates and other investment documents should be properly controlled by authorized personnel and bankers or brokers, if any.

Associated
Materials   Safekeeping Receipt Form (Figure 2-1)

Procedures   **Investments Held by Authorized Agent**

2.1   Certain investments may be held by an authorized agent dependent upon the type of investment activity. For instance, banks may or may not issue passbooks or certificates for demand and time deposits. Investments of this type should be held in a separate account, the activity of which will be reported on a periodic statement. In addition, other investments such as bonds, notes, or stock certificates may be physically controlled by a broker, bank, or bank trust department. If investments are held by an unrelated organization, a safekeeping receipt should be received in support of each transaction (Figure 2-1).

Investment Certificate or Safekeeping Receipt

2.2   An investment certificate or safekeeping receipt and a statement should be received in exchange for the check or bank transfer. For purposes of this section, an investment certificate refers to any evidence of investment including savings account passbooks, certificates of deposit, notes, bonds, stock certificates, and so on.

Investment Control Log

2.3 The investment certificate statement or safekeeping receipt may not be received until several days after the settlement date. Therefore, purchases in progress should be recorded on the investment control log (Figure 1-1). The investment control log should be updated with each change in status (i.e. trade date, settlement date, when the certificate or safekeeping receipt is received, etc.).

Physical Safeguards

2.4 All investment certificates kept on the company's premises should be physically safeguarded against theft, loss, misuse, or damage. The certificates should be kept in a locked, fireproof safe. If a safe is not available, a locked file cabinet should be utilized for temporary storage. Regardless of the storage facility used, it should be accessible only to authorized personnel. In addition, the safe should be opened only by authorized personnel, when accompanied by an authorized witness.

Investment Access Control Log

2.5 An investment access control log should be established and maintained. Such a log documents the important data regarding the safekeeping access, including date, time, personnel, witness, documents accessed, and so on.

Investment Storage Facility

2.6 If the company does not have a suitable investment storage facility on site, then arrangements should be made to rent a safety deposit box at a financial institution. The safety deposit box should be accessible only when two authorized personnel are present. A safekeeping access control log as described in section 2.4 should be utilized.

Preparation of Investment File

2.7 The company should prepare an investment file for each investment. The file, established when the investment number is assigned, should contain the following documents:
- Original investment authorization form
- Copy of the check request
- Copy of the investment certificate, statements, or original safekeeping receipt forms
- Purchase and sale correspondence, communications, etc.
- Copy of the deposit ticket/receipt for sales proceeds

- Copy of the investment gain/loss calculations
- Copy of the interest income or dividend earnings worksheet
- Copy of the premium/discount amortization calculations

SECTION VIII
FIGURE 2-1

Safekeeping Receipt Form

Date _____

From   XYZ Company _____

We received/released (description of security) _____
_____
_____
_____

Security was received/delivered from/to _____
_____
_____

Authorized Signature _____

Title _____

3. *RETURN ON INVESTMENT*

Policy   Earnings on investments should be calculated and recorded in the general ledger monthly.

General   Separate investment income accounts should be utilized to record monthly activity. Such accounts should include interest and dividend accruals, and related interest and dividend income accounts as well as accounts for both the unamortized balance and the current year amortization of investment premiums and discounts. Such accounts should distinguish between taxable and nontaxable amounts.

Associated Materials   Interest Income Worksheet (Figure 3-1)
Dividend Earnings Worksheet (Figure 3-2)

Procedures   **Interest Income**

3.1   Interest income should be recorded monthly for earnings on all investments. The earnings should be calculated for each investment and aggregated for recording purposes. A worksheet similar to that in Figure 3-1 should be used to document the interest income calculations.

Common/Preferred Stock

3.2   A worksheet similar to Figure 3-2 should be utilized to summarize earnings on common and preferred stock investments. This worksheet should also be utilized to record dividends receivable at month end, if any. Dividends are receivable on the record date, the date an owner becomes legally entitled to receive the dividend, and should be recorded at that time.
Stock shares received as a result of a stock dividend should be recorded as earnings, calculated based on the fair value of the stock on the record date. Stock shares received as a result of a stock split

should not result in earnings but will result in a reduction of the historical cost per share.

Premium/Discount on Bonds and Notes Receivable

3.3 Certain bonds and notes receivable can be acquired and sold at amounts other than face value. The amount in excess of face value is a premium whereas the amount of the reduction from face value is a discount. The premium or discount represents the present value of the future amounts necessary to adjust the stated interest rate to a market rate on the trade date. The amount of the premium represents a reduction of earnings calculated at the stated rate and should be recognized over the investment holding period. Similarly, a discount represents additional earnings that should be recognized over the investment holding period.

Premiums and discounts should be amortized into income utilizing the interest method. The interest method results in a level yield on each investment over the applicable holding period.

Investment Income Schedule

3.4 A schedule should be prepared to support the various investment income and premium/discount general ledger accounts. The schedule should be similar to Figures 3-1 and 3-2 and will include:
- investment number;
- investment description;
- date acquired;
- interest rate, if applicable;
- face amount;
- historical cost;
- amortization/adjustments to date;
- carrying value.

Investment Summary Schedule

3.5 A summary schedule of the total activity by investment type should be prepared as indicated in 1.8.

Proper Valuation of "Marketable Equity Securities"

3.6 A valuation account should be established to capture and record the difference between cost and market value of all "marketable equity securities" in the aggregate. Subsequent adjustments (recoveries or declines) should be recorded in a timely fashion.

SECTION VIII
FIGURE 3-1

XYZ Company
Interest Income Worksheet
March, 199X

Investment Number	Description	Date Acquired Month/Year	Interest Rate	Face Amount	Interest Accrual at 2/29/9X	Earnings	Receipts	Interest Accrual at 3/31/9X
	Certificates of Deposit							
2473	Star Bank CD	10/9X	7.25	10,000	1,208.33	604.17	1,812.50	0
	Etc.							

SECTION VIII
FIGURE 3-2

XYZ Company
Dividend Earnings Worksheet
November 19, 199X

Investment Number	Description	Record Date	Dividend Per Share	Number of Shares	Dividends Receivable at 10/31/9X	Dividends Earned	Received	Dividends Received at 11/30/9X
2326	ABC Co. Common	11/16	.35	2,000	0	700		700
2472	J Preferred	10/25	.10	5,000	500		500	0
2501	SFD Common	11/2	.50	4,000	0	2,000	2,000	0
	Total				500	2,700	2,500	700

4. *INVESTMENTS WITH SIGNIFICANT INFLUENCE*

Policy The equity method should be used to account for investments in common stock in which the company exercises "significant influence" over the investee corporation.

General The provisions of Accounting Principles Board (APB) Opinion No. 18— Equity Method of Accounting for Investments in Common Stock should be applied to the company's investments in:

- unconsolidated subsidiaries,
- corporate joint ventures, and
- other investments of 50 percent or less of the voting stock of the investee corporation where the company can exert "significant influence."

Refer to APB Opinion No. 18 for guidance in determining applicable investments.

Associated Materials None

Procedures **Equity Method of Accounting**

4.1 All voting stock investments should be reviewed by the treasurer or his or her designee to determine if the equity method of accounting is applicable.

Investee Corporation Earnings

4.2 For applicable investments, identified in 4.1, a proportionate share of the investee corporation earnings should be recorded in the income statement each month. The amount to be recorded is determined by multiplying the ownership percentage times the net income of the investee corporation for the current period. Any amounts recognized should increase the investment account. A similar adjustment is necessary to recognize current period losses. However, the investment account should not have a credit balance due to continued losses of an investee corporation. Once the investment account is reduced to zero the proportionate share of net losses (unless guaranteed by the company) should not be recognized in the income statement. Any dividends received from the investee corporation should be credited against the investment account.

Section IX

PROPERTY, PLANT, AND EQUIPMENT

```
┌─────────────────────────────────────────────────────────────┐
│  _____      _____       │
│  Company Name                          Date                   │
│                                                               │
│  _____                            │
│  Approval                                                     │
└─────────────────────────────────────────────────────────────┘
```

1. *ADDITIONS TO PROPERTY, PLANT, AND EQUIPMENT*

Policy　All additions to property, plant, and equipment should be properly authorized. Expenditures for tangible assets used actively in business operations that benefit a period exceeding one fiscal year should be capitalized. (It should be noted that record-keeping expediency and income tax regulations permit expensing capital asset costs of relatively small individual amounts such as less than $500.)

General　Property, plant, and equipment are generally categorized by the following broad asset types:

- Land
- Buildings and production facilities
- Machinery and equipment
- Furniture, fixtures, and office equipment
- Leasehold improvements
- Computer equipment, including purchased software
- Tools and dies
- Property subject to depletion, including oil wells, mines, and timber
- Construction in progress
- Automobiles and transportation equipment
- Equipment leased to others

Capital budgeting is as integral to forming a company's annual business plan as is operations budgeting. Since the budgeting process must take place far in advance, estimations of acquisitions in the budget year must be made. The decision to purchase a capital asset should be an informed one based on current year budgets, projected benefits of the addition, and analysis of the lease versus purchase option.

Associated Materials　Appropriations Request Form (Figure 1-1)

Procedures **Approval of Capital Budgeting**

1.1 Capital budgets should be submitted along with operating budgets for review and approval by the appropriate levels of management.

Capital Asset Purchase Authorizations

1.2 No purchase of capital assets should be made without proper authorization and review to ensure compliance with budget guidelines and sound investment decision making.

Approval of Appropriation Requests

1.3 Appropriation requests (Figure 1-1) should be submitted and approved by appropriate levels of management as determined by the dollar magnitude of the acquisition before funds are committed for capital expenditures.

(a) Appropriation requests should be required for all capital assets expenditures for which the cost exceeds a record-keeping dollar threshold, for example, $500.

(b) The request should specify the reason for the request and the estimated cost.

(c) In some instances, capital items will need to be purchased that were not included in the budget. The appropriations request form should be completed for these types of purchases also.

Long-Term Lease or Purchase

1.4 Obtaining the use of property, plant, and equipment through long-term leases is an alternative to outright purchase. Leases vary in term, assumption of expenses, and many other details. The purchase-versus-lease decision should be based upon the basis of net cost, considering:
- cash-flow consideration,
- tax treatment,
- financial statement presentation, and
- suitability of the asset to leasing (i.e., some assets, such as computers, are subject to rapid technological change and may not be of as much benefit to the company after a few years).

SECTION IX
FIGURE 1-1

Appropriations Request Form

Appropriation # _____

Description of
Expenditure _____

Department to Be
Charged _____

Cash Requirements _____ (a)

Budgeted Amount _____ (b)

*Present Value of
Discounted
Cash Flows _____

Over (Under)
Budget _____ (a – b)

# of Other
Attachments _____

Date Cash
Is Needed _____

_____
(Authorizing Signature)

_____
(Title)

_____
(Date)

*To assist in determining whether a lease should be capitalized and the proper recording thereof.

<table>
<tr><td>Company Name</td><td>Date</td></tr>
<tr><td colspan="2">Approval</td></tr>
</table>

2. *ACCURATE RECORDS OF PROPERTY, PLANT, AND EQUIPMENT*

Policy   Accurate records should be maintained of the cost and accumulated depreciation of property, plant, and equipment.

General   The acquisition of capital assets should be organized to ensure that no unauthorized acquisitions have been made and that records of each acquisition are accurate, complete, and recorded in the appropriate period.

Associated Materials   Detailed Fixed Asset Ledger (Figure 2-1)

Procedures   **Receipt and Identification of Capital Assets**

2.1   See Section X—3.0 regarding the receipt of capital assets. In addition, all property and plant items should be identified upon their receipt by the use of a prenumbered tag:
- The tag should be permanently affixed in a readily visible area.
- The property number on the tag should be recorded in the detailed fixed asset ledger.
- The location of the asset installation should be recorded in the detailed fixed asset ledger.

Review of Purchase Price Variances

2.2   For each capital item purchased, a comparison should be made of the actual versus budgeted cost. Differences should be explained and approved by a responsible official.

Maintenance of Detailed Fixed Asset Ledgers

2.3   Detailed fixed asset ledgers (Figure 2-1) that are accurate and complete should be maintained for the following classifications:

- Land and buildings
- Oil wells, mines and timber
- Leasehold improvements
- Plant equipment and machinery
- Furniture and fixtures
- Office equipment
- Motor vehicles
- Other
- Assets leased from or loaned to third parties

Depreciable Assets Net Acquisition Costs

2.4 Depreciable assets should be carried in the accounting records at the original net acquisition cost, less separate accounts for accumulated depreciation or depletion. Nondepreciable capital assets (e.g., land) customarily should be carried in the records at the original net cost. Purchased items of property, plant, and equipment that meet the capitalization requirements are to be capitalized at the invoice price plus all charges incurred to prepare the asset for operations.

2.4.1 Cost of acquisition or construction includes not only the contract or invoice price but also such costs as preliminary engineering studies and surveys, legal fees to establish title, installation costs, sales tax, freight, and labor and material used in construction or installation.

2.4.2 Cash discounts taken should be recorded as a reduction of the cost.

Posting to Detailed Ledger

2.5 Asset additions, disposals, and period depreciation should be posted to the detailed ledger regularly.

Reconciliation to General Ledger

2.6 On a periodic basis, the detailed fixed asset ledger should be reconciled with the general ledger for asset cost and accumulated depreciation.

Investigation and Resolution of Differences

2.7 Any differences disclosed by the reconciliation in 2.6 should be investigated and resolved.

Review of Differences

2.8 The results of the reconciliation should be reviewed and approved by a responsible employee before any adjustments to the account are recorded. Such review should be evidenced by a signature.

Capitalization of Expenditures While Building

2.9 Expenditures made by the company while building a capital asset should be capitalized.

2.9.1 Expenditures such as those for materials, labor, engineering, supervision, clerks' salaries and expenses, legal expenses, insurance, overhead, and interest should be capitalized as "construction in progress" until the project is completed and placed in service. No depreciation should be taken on construction in progress.

2.9.2 Periodically during construction, a comparison should be made between projected and actual expenses incurred. Appropriate approvals should be obtained if projected costs will exceed the budgeted amount.

2.9.3 Upon completion of construction and placement in service, the asset should be removed from construction in progress and entered into the detailed fixed asset ledger under the appropriate classification. Depreciation should now be taken on the asset.

Expenditures—Capitalization vs. Expense

2.10 Repair expense should be distinguished from expenditures for improvements, additions, renovations, alterations, and replacements.

(a) Expenditures are repair expense if they do not materially add to the value of the property and do not materially prolong the life of the property. Examples of repair expense:

- Replacing loose or damaged shingles
- Replacing broken glass
- Painting and decorating a showroom
- Resurfacing a parking lot
- Making temporary repairs to last less than one year
- Making minor repairs to fully depreciated assets

(b) Repair costs that increase the value of property, prolong its life, or adapt it to a new or different use are capital expenditures. If the life of the asset has been significantly extended, the remaining original cost and the repair cost should be depreciated over the new life. Examples of repair expenditures that are capital expenditures:

- Replacing floors
- Replacing a roof, thereby substantially prolonging its life
- Reconditioning machinery, thereby extending its life
- Replacing an auto's or a truck's engine
- Overhauling an auto or truck that was substantially worn out
- Installing a new heating system

(c) Other expenditures that may be capitalized:

- Land improvements that depreciate over time (e.g., parking lots)
- Structural changes or alterations to company-owned buildings, which become a part of a building and increase its life or value
- Significant improvements to property leased by the company, improvements that add value to the leasehold (e.g., permanent office partitions)

SECTION IX
FIGURE 2-1

Detailed Fixed Asset Ledger

Prepared by	...../...../.....
Approved by	...../...../.....

Company ....
Year end: ..../...../.........

	DATE	CLASSIFICATION	1 BALANCE AT BEGINNING OF PERIOD	2 ADDITIONS	3 DISPOSALS	4 OTHER	5 BALANCE AT END OF PERIOD
1		ASSET					
2							
3							
4							
5							
6							
7							
8							
9							
10							
11							
12							
13							
14							
15							
16							
17							
18							
19							
20							
21							
22							
23							
24							
25							
26							
27							
28							
29							
30							
31							
32							
33							
34							
35							
36							

		CLASSIFICATION	BALANCE AT BEGINNING OF PERIOD	ADDITIONS	DISPOSALS	OTHER	BALANCE AT END OF PERIOD
			1	2	3	4	5
1		ACCUMULATED DEPRECIATION					
2							
3							
4							
5							
6							
7							
8							
9							
10							
11							
12							
13							
14							
15							
16							
17							
18							
19							
20							
21							
22							
23							
24							
25							
26							
27							
28							
29							
30							
31							
32							
33							
34							
35							
36							

Company Name	Date
Approval	

3. *DEPRECIATION OF PROPERTY, PLANT, AND EQUIPMENT*

Policy The cost (less salvage value) of all capitalizable assets should be allocated (depreciated) over the estimated useful lives in a rational and systematic manner.

General Four generally accepted depreciation methods can be used to systematically allocate an asset's cost (less salvage value) over its useful life:

- Straight line—an equal amount of the net cost of an asset allocated to each accounting period in its useful life.
- Declining balance—a larger portion of the asset's net cost in the earlier periods of its useful life and a smaller amount in the later periods.
- Sum of the year's digits—another accelerated method of depreciation whereby a larger portion of the asset's net cost is allocated to earlier periods and a smaller amount in later periods.
- Units of production or hours of service—the asset's net cost is allocated to each accounting period based on the productivity or length of service of the asset. (Depletion is calculated in a manner similar to the units of production method.)

Associated Materials None

Procedures **Determination of Useful Life**

3.1 The useful life should be determined when a capital asset is acquired. The useful life may be expressed in terms of time, units of production, or hours of service.

(a)   The cost of an asset should be allocated over a useful life via depreciation or depletion.

(b)   When a useful life is not determinable, such as for land, no depreciation should be taken.

(c)   If there is a change in the estimate of the remaining useful life after the asset is placed into service, the remaining cost to be depreciated should be spread over the revised remaining life.

(d)   The estimated useful life should be reviewed by an appropriate level of management.

Determination of Depreciation Method

3.2   A responsible management employee should determine the method of depreciation to be used for each category of capital assets.

(a)   The justification for the method selected should be well documented and maintained. Accelerated methods are used in situations where an asset's physical usefulness or value declines quickly in the earlier years (e.g., computers).

(b)   Once a sound depreciation method has been selected, it should be applied consistently until conditions change to such a degree that its application no longer produces reasonable results.

(c)   Circumstances may arise that make it appropriate to accelerate or decelerate depreciation charges:
   • A change in the estimate of the useful life.
   • A change in the estimated salvage value. This is a change in accounting estimate that should be accounted for prospectively, not retroactively, by depreciating the remaining balance over the remaining useful life.
   • A change in depreciation method.

Tax Deferrals Through Accelerated Depreciation Methods

3.3   For tax reporting purposes, the company may elect to defer tax payments through the use of accelerated methods of depreciation different than the method used for financial statement reporting. A separate fixed asset ledger prepared on a tax basis should be maintained.

```
┌──────────────────────────────────────────────────────────┐
│  _____        _____ │
│  Company Name                       Date                    │
│  _____                                │
│  Approval                                                   │
└──────────────────────────────────────────────────────────┘
```

4. EXISTENCE OF CAPITAL ASSETS

Policy   Control should be maintained over capital assets and their related records to ensure that all recorded assets exist and are in use for operations.

General   The physical existence of capital assets should be verified and reconciled to the fixed asset records.

Associated Materials   None

Procedures   **Identification and Record of Assets**

4.1   At the time of acquisition, all assets should have been identified, tagged, and entered into the detailed fixed asset ledger. The tag should have been placed in a visible area. The tags provide a clear method of tracing the asset on the floor to the fixed asset ledger.

      Periodically, the company should take a physical inventory of all capital assets to ensure the completeness and accuracy of the company's records.

(a)   The inventory process should be overseen by responsible management employees who are not responsible for the custody or record keeping of the assets.

(b)   All assets should be examined to determine that they are currently being used.

Comparison to Detailed Records

4.2   The inventory of the assets on hand should be compared to the detailed records.

Resolution of Differences

4.3   All differences should be resolved by a responsible management employee.

5. *DISPOSAL OF CAPITAL ASSETS*

Policy   Disposal of capital assets should occur only after proper authorization has been given.

General   Control over the disposition of property should be maintained not only to preserve the accuracy of the records but also to ensure that assets are safeguarded, improper disposal is avoided, and the best possible terms are received for disposal.

**Associated
Materials**   Disposal Form (Figure 5-1)

Procedures   **Documentation of Disposal**

5.1   The following procedures should apply to the retirement and disposal of company assets:

(a)   No item of property, plant, and equipment should be removed from the premises without a properly approved disposal form (Figure 5-1).

(b)   A disposal form should be completed for all disposals.

(c)   This disposal form should be reviewed and approved by a responsible employee who is knowledgeable and not directly responsible for the asset.

Recording Disposal

5.2   Once the retirement has been properly approved and documented, the following procedures apply to the recording of the transaction:

(a)   At the time the property is retired, the cost should be removed from the appropriate asset account; the related accumulated depreciation, including depreciation to date of disposal, should be removed from the allowance for depreciation account; and the profit or loss, adjusted for the cost of removal, should be recorded as an income (gain) or expense (loss) item.

(b)   When the disposal is via a trade-in of a similar asset, the acquired asset should be recorded at the book value of the trade-in asset plus any additional cash paid. In no instance should such cost exceed the fair market value for the new asset.

Fully Depreciated Assets

5.3   Fully depreciated assets should remain on the property records with the related accumulated depreciation as long as the property is still in use.

SECTION IX
FIGURE 5-1

Disposal Form

Company _____

Tag # of Property Disposed	_____		Reason for Disposal	_____

Description _____ _____
_____

Year of Acquisition _____

Original Cost _____ (a)   Tax Basis _____ (d)   ITC Recapture _____

Accumulated Depreciation _____ (b)   Tax Accumulated Depreciation _____ (e)

Net Book Value _____ (a – b)   Tax Net Book Value _____ (d – e)

Proceeds/Scrap Value* _____ (c)   Proceeds/Scrap Value* _____ (f)

Book (Gain) Loss _____ (a – b – c)   Tax (Gain) Loss _____ (d – e – f)

*Net of disposal costs.

_____
(Authorizing Signature)
_____
(Title)
_____
(Date)

Section X

PURCHASING CYCLE

```
┌─────────────────────────────────────────────────────────────┐
│  _____      _____       │
│  Company Name                          Date                   │
│  _____                             │
│  Approval                                                     │
└─────────────────────────────────────────────────────────────┘
```

1. *DETERMINATION OF NEEDS*

Policy Determination of company needs for goods and services should be made by appropriate personnel and according to company guidelines.

General The determination of needs for goods and services, such as raw material inventory, equipment, office supplies, and professional services, should be made by qualified individuals in the company and according to organizational guidelines that consider adequate quantities, reasonable prices, timely receipt, proper specifications, and desired quality. The guidelines must also consider and avoid the disruption of operational efficiency because of improper or untimely purchases and potential losses and use of cash caused by excessive purchases.

Associated Materials Requisition Form (Figure 1-1)

Procedures **Methods to Determine Needs**

   1.1   Purchasing requirements, categorized by the type of goods or service, should be determined according to the following methods:

   (a)   Raw material inventory replenishment needs should be determined: by a supervisor who has responsibility for the specific task, automatically when stock on hand reaches a reorder point, per a bill of materials for a job order.

   (b)   The need for services that are provided on a recurring basis by the same vendor, such as utilities, telephone, periodicals, or janitorial services, should be determined initially by authorized persons and, thereafter, provided continuously or not redetermined until the end of the contract period.

   (c)   Determining the need for specialized services, such as insurance, advertising, and legal and accounting services, should be the responsibility of designated individuals or committees.

(d)   The need for occasional goods and services should be identified by the user and approved by a responsible person, such as a supervisor, director of manufacturing, office manager, and so on.

Preparation of Requisitions for Routine Goods and Services

1.2   Requisitions (Figure 1-1) for routine goods and services (items that are commonly used in the production of the company's products or resale activity if the company is a wholesaler or retailer, including administrative support items) should be prepared by the user department and contain the following information:

(a)   Vendor—name and address of vendor if it is appropriate for user department to specify the vendor from which they desire to purchase the product or service.

(b)   Billing address—specific location where invoices should be sent.

(c)   Date requested—date that requisition was made by user department.

(d)   Date required—specific date that items requested are needed. Always estimate or project a specific preferred date the material or service is to be delivered. This consideration will assist the purchasing department in determining priorities. Always provide as much lead time as practical by determining your needs as far as possible in advance. Denote "RUSH" when relevant to alert the purchasing personnel of the need for prompt action or priority of purchase. The supervisor of each department, or designee, is responsible for requisitioning materials or services in sufficient time to allow purchasing to transact and arrange shipment and/or delivery in the most cost-efficient manner.

(e)   Ship or deliver to—specific location where goods or services are to be delivered.

(f)   Ship via—if appropriate the user department indicates the transportation or freight carrier, otherwise, the means of shipment is determined by the purchasing department.

(g)   On arrival notify—name of originator or individual designated to receive goods when received from vendor.

(h)   Item—list in numeric sequence (if part numbers are used) each separate item to be purchased.

(i)   Quantity—specific quantity to be purchased and delivered.

(j)   Unit of measure—unit of measure is important and should be entered to assist the purchasing department.

(k)   Description—specific description of items ordered, including part number, name, catalog number, reference, model number, color, dimensions, and so on.

(l)   Unit price—list current unit price, if known.

(m)   Requested by—name of individual submitting the requisition.

(n)   Approval—signature and date of individual authorized to approve expenditure.

(o)   Purchase order number—assigned by the purchasing department (see 2.4).

(p)   Control number—number used to identify specific requisition. Form may be prenumbered.

Initiation of Requisitions for Specialized Services

1.3   Requisitions for specialized services typically should be initiated by individuals authorized to make the specific type of purchase. If the purchase is to be for goods or services that can be requested on the requisition form described in 1.2, the requisition form should be used. If the goods or services are complex, highly technical, or require a formal request for proposal or contract, the appropriate contract or document should be prepared by an authorized individual. Review and approval of the document or contract should be approved by the following, as deemed appropriate by the company:

- Authorized supervisor or department head
- Authorized company officer
- Committee formed or authorized to commit to such a purchase
- Board of directors
- Company's legal counsel

Initiation of Requisitions for Plant, Property, and Equipment

1.4   Requisitions for fixed asset additions should be initiated by the user departments and in accordance with a capital budgeting process. When possible, a requisition form, as described in 1.2, should be used. Approval should be received from the supervisor or company officer responsible for such a purchase. Significant purchases should be approved by the board of directors.

Limitation on Purchases Through Imprest Funds

1.5   Purchases through an imprest fund should be limited to a specific dollar limit, for items that are purchased in small quantities and usually require a purchase within a very short time period. Companies typically use a petty cash fund for such purchases, and a petty cash voucher is filled out for each purchase and given to the person responsible for keeping the petty cash fund. The practice of making voluminous purchases through the imprest fund is discouraged (see IV—4.0).

SECTION X
FIGURE 1-1

Requisition Form

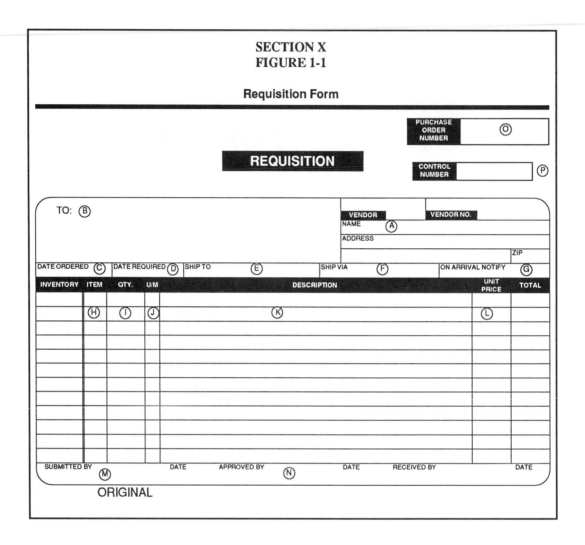

2. *PLACEMENT OF ORDERS*

Policy   Proper approval should be obtained prior to the establishment of a firm order or contract to purchase. Administrative control should be established over orders placed.

General   Requisitions for purchases should be reviewed to ascertain that the amount of requisition is within the approved company limit. Purchase orders should be made on approved purchase order forms and reviewed for correctness. Approval of the purchase orders per company guidelines should be received prior to establishment of a firm order or contract. Copies of the purchase orders should be filed to allow for timely follow-up on uncompleted orders.

Associated Materials   Approval Limit Schedule (Figure 2-1)
Purchase Order (Figure 2-2)

Procedures   **Capable Purchasing Personnel**

2.1   The company should have capable purchasing personnel. For most enterprises of sufficient size, administrative control is enhanced if trained purchasing agents, rather than personnel from user departments, determine sources, negotiate terms, and place orders. A separate purchasing function increases the efficiency and effectiveness of a business.

Establishment of Purchasing Guidelines

2.2   Purchasing guidelines that define approval requirements and procedures for purchase commitments should be determined by the president or an officer designated by the president. The purchasing guidelines should contain the following items, as applicable:

(a)   Approval limits (see Figure 2-1 for example of approval limit schedule) over which the buyer is required to obtain appropriate approval prior to the establishment of a firm order or contract.

(b) Fixed asset appropriation requests for all such expenditures over a specified dollar amount prior to commitment of funds.

(c) Purchases against approved capital appropriations that require approval by the department head responsible for the project.

(d) Purchases for certain specialized goods and services that require technical expertise. However, these situations should be limited.

Entering Into Purchase Commitments

2.3 The company should consider entering into purchase commitments. For example, the company may enter a contract to purchase a certain amount of material over a specified period of time. These purchase commitments may be entered into to assure an adequate supply or price. All contracts should be documented in writing and the approval of the top officers should be obtained before a firm contract is signed. Furthermore, in order to avoid losses from inappropriate commitments, a very sophisticated projection of the company's requirements for the specified goods or services should be prepared.

Preparation of Prenumbered Purchase Orders

2.4 Prenumbered purchase orders (see Figure 2-2) should be prepared and contain the following information, as applicable:

(a) Name and address of vendor

(b) Ship-to information (location)

(c) Date the order was placed

(d) Date the goods are to be delivered or service performed

(e) Mode of transportation

(f) Terms of purchase (i.e., down payment, returnable if not used, etc.)

(g) Each item listed separately with description

(h) Specific quantity and unit of measure

(i) Unit price

(j) Signature of authorized buyer

Reviewing for Accuracy

2.5 Before the purchase orders are released, the following review steps for accuracy should be made:
- Dates and quantities reconciled to requisition
- Prices compared to masterfiles or standards
- Extensions and footings checked

Multiple-Copy Purchase Order Forms

2.6 Multiple-copy purchase order forms should be used, with copies being distributed as follows:
- Original to vendor
- Purchasing department tickler file to allow follow-up on a timely basis for shipments or orders not received on a specified date
- Accounts payable department
- Receiving department to be used to verify and check goods received

Review of Unmatched Purchase Commitments

2.7 On a periodic basis, a review should be performed of any commitments that have not been matched with receiving reports or equivalent records of goods or services received.

Approval of Review

2.8 The results in 2.7 should be reviewed and approved by a responsible official.

SECTION X
FIGURE 2-1

Approval Limit Schedule

Company Name

SPENDING AUTHORIZATION LIMITS

Effective _____
Date

(in Thousands)

Dollar Limits	.5	1	2	3	5	10	25
President	X	X	X	X	X	X	X
Vice-Presidents	X	X	X	X	X	X	
Directors	X	X	X	X	X	X	
General Managers (Purchasing Supervisor)	X	X					
Asst. General Managers	X						
Managers	X						
Supervisors	X						

SECTION X
FIGURE 2-2

Purchase Order

PURCHASE ORDER

32071

ABOVE ORDER NO. MUST
APPEAR ON ALL PAPERS
AND PACKAGES RELATIVE
TO THIS ORDER, INCLUD-
ING CORRESPONDENCE

INVOICE IN TRIPLICATE TO

☐ SEE ABOVE ☐ SAME AS SHIP TO BELOW

VENDOR Ⓐ

SHIP TO Ⓑ

REQUISITIONER DEPARTMENT

ORDER DATE Ⓒ	ENGAGEMENT NUMBER	SHIP VIA Ⓔ	PAYMENT TERMS Ⓕ	DELIVERY DATE Ⓓ

ITEM NO.	QUANTITY	DESCRIPTION	UNIT PRICE	TOTAL
	Ⓗ	Ⓖ	Ⓘ	

BY _____ Ⓙ

AUTHORIZED SIGNATURE

3. *RECEIPT AND ACCEPTANCE*

Policy Control should be established over goods and services received as a basis for determining and recording the liability for goods and services received.

General The physical receipt of all purchased goods should be the responsibility of a receiving department or designated individual. The receiving function should inspect goods for conformity with specifications on purchase orders. Quantities should be verified by counting, weighing, or measuring. Receipt and acceptance of a shipment should be documented on a receiving report (or on a copy of the purchase order utilized for such purpose) with copies of the receiving reports being routed to the purchasing and accounting departments.

Associated Materials Receiving Report—Description and Quantity Manually Written (Figure 3-1)
Receiving Report—Copy of Purchase Order Used (Figure 3-2)
Receiving Control Log (Figure 3-3)

Procedures **Inspection of All Goods and Services**

3.1 A receiving department or designated individual should inspect all goods received. If the size of the company permits, the receiving department should be separate from the requisitioning, purchasing, and accounting departments. Depending upon the specialization or technical knowledge needed to inspect the goods received, the company should determine if it is practical for the receiving department to make the total detailed inspection of goods. If it is decided to have the receiving department make the total inspection of goods, the following inspection procedures should be performed:

3.1.1 Upon receipt of any item, the following immediate action should occur:
- Check the bill of lading for the correct delivery point.
- Verify the number of containers with the bill of lading.

- Examine containers for exterior damage.
- Note on the bill of lading any discrepancy (i.e., missing containers, damage, etc.).
- Sign and date the bill of lading.
- Retain a copy for the receiving department.

3.1.2 When goods are moved to another area for thorough inspection, the following inspection procedures should be performed:

- Remove the packing slip from the container.
- Remove from the receiving department file the corresponding purchase order.
- Compare the description of goods and quantity per the purchase order to the packing slip. (Note: This is performed when the receiving department is given total information on its copy of the purchase order, which is not advisable.)
- Examine goods for physical damage.
- Count or weigh items. Similarly packaged items may be counted on a test basis, if deemed appropriate. If goods are of a high dollar value and subject to breakage from shipment, the company may want all goods counted and tested upon receipt to avoid delays in production when parts are found to be defective.
- Make an indication of the counts on the copy of the purchase order. The inspection process should be timely. Delays in inspection can cause delays in production due to material shortages, and inaccurate accounting information can be caused by inventory and accounts payable not being recorded on a timely basis.

Proper Communication Between Departments

3.2 The receiving department should contact the purchasing department if any order has an obvious discrepancy (physical damage, wrong item delivered, quantity error, etc.). The purchasing department should notify the vendor and in an expeditious manner give the receiving department direction regarding the disposition.

Preparation of Receiving Request

3.3 A receiving report (Figures 3-1 and 3-2) should be prepared. The receiving report should be designed to the company's specific requirements. There are several alternatives for the format of a receiving document:

- A copy of the purchase order
- A copy of the purchase order with quantities omitted to improve the likelihood of independent verification or count of quantities
- A separate receiving document requiring the receiving department to manually provide a written description of goods and quantities

Regardless of the format, the receiving document should contain the following information:

(a) Prenumber. Receiving documents should be printed with sequential numbering. This is extremely important in gaining control over all receiving documents written.

(b) Date of receipt.

(c) Incompleteness. In the event goods received are less than the full amount purchased, the incompleteness should be noted on the receiving report. A copy of the incomplete purchase order should be retained by the receiving department until such time as it is complete.

(d) Signature of employee in charge of making inspection.

Receiving Documentation Filed in Receiving and Sent to Purchasing

3.4 After inspection, the receiving report, with the attached copy of the purchase order, the packing slip, and the bill of lading, should be sent to the purchasing department. A copy of the receiving report and the related purchase order should be filed in the receiving department. The receiving department file of receiving reports is an important aid in attaining proper purchase cut-off at the end of an accounting period (see 6.0) and in determining if there are misplaced receiving reports and/or unrecorded receipts.

Inspection and Approval of All Services Received

3.5 Services that are received should also be inspected or reviewed by the user department to determine that the work was done in accordance with the purchase order or contract. Approval by the user department should be documented on the purchase order copy or stated in memo form and sent to the purchasing department.

If the work is of a confidential or highly technical nature, the company may desire to have an officer of the company review the documentation for inspection and approval of services received.

Storing and Controlling of Goods

3.6 Raw materials, component parts, and other goods should be accounted for and controlled from the time of receipt through utilization. With the increased use of the "just-in-time" manufacturing concept, many companies have goods routed directly from receiving to the user departments. Such an operating procedure reduces the number of non-value-added steps in a company's operations. However, if this procedure is used, the company should ensure that the goods are protected from the elements and possible misuse in the user department. Any transfers to the appropriate user department should be noted on the receiving report.

If the company's operations are such that goods are sent directly to a central storeroom area from receiving, such a transfer should be noted on the receiving report. The central storeroom area should have the following procedures to account for and control the goods:

(a)   Access to the storeroom should be restricted to authorized personnel.

(b)   Materials should be issued from the storeroom only on receipt of one of the following documents:

1. An authorized bill of material supporting an approved production order
2. Report of production orders scheduled to start
3. An approved materials requisition

In any event, an appropriately authorized document should be created to account for the movement of materials, both for production control and accounting purposes. These documents serve as authorization to update perpetual inventory records for issues of material to production and should be prenumbered or subject to some type of batch control so that it can be ascertained that all transactions have been processed and recorded.

Comparison of Receiving Log to Receiving Reports

3.7   The purchasing department should keep a list or log of receiving reports (Figure 3-3) received and processed and should account for numerical sequence. Periodically, this list should be compared to the file of receiving reports kept in the receiving department. Differences should be investigated. A journal entry should be prepared to record receiving reports for goods that have been received prior to the end of an accounting period but have not been matched with the related suppliers' invoices. See 6.0 for further discussion of cut-off procedures at the end of an accounting period.

Approval and Review of Discrepancies in 3.7

3.8   The results of the procedures in 3.7 should be reviewed and approved by a responsible official.

SECTION X
FIGURE 3-1

Receiving Report—description and quantity manually written

RECEIVING RECORD   (A) 74914

RECEIVED
FROM:

DATE _____ (B) _____
PO NO. _____
PS NO. _____

Vendor # _____

#	Qty.	Part No.	Description	Account	Price

Comments: _____

_____ (C) _____ _____

POSTED BY: _____ DELIVER TO: _____

INSPECTED BY: _____ (D) _____ DATE: _____

SECTION X
FIGURE 3-2

Receiving Report—Copy of Purchase Order Used

PURCHASE ORDER

(A) 32071

ABOVE ORDER NO. MUST APPEAR ON ALL PAPERS AND PACKAGES RELATIVE TO THIS ORDER, INCLUDING CORRESPONDENCE

INVOICE IN TRIPLICATE TO

☐ SEE ABOVE   ☐ SAME AS SHIP TO BELOW

VENDOR   **SHIP TO**

REQUISITIONER   DEPARTMENT

ORDER DATE	ENGAGEMENT NUMBER	SHIP VIA	PAYMENT TERMS	DELIVERY DATE
ITEM NO.	QUANTITY	DESCRIPTION	UNIT PRICE	TOTAL

BY (D)

_____

AUTHORIZED SIGNATURE

DATE	NO.	Quan. Rec'd.	Bal. Due	QUALITY	Inspected By	DATE	NO.	Quan. Rec'd.	Bal. Due	QUALITY	Inspected By
(B)			(C)		(D)						

RECEIVING LOG

DATE _____

Rec. No.	P.O. #	Vendor	Description	Quantity

4. *ESTABLISHMENT OF ACCOUNTS PAYABLE*

Policy All valid accounts payable transactions, and only those transactions, should be accurately recorded as accounts payable.

General The recording of assets or expenses and the related liability should be recorded by employees independent of the ordering and receiving functions, where the size of the company allows for this segregation of duties. The amounts recorded should be based on vendor invoices for the related goods or services. The vendor invoices should be in agreement with an approved purchase order. Furthermore, evidence of receipt or performance should be in the form of a receiving report or other approved documentation before the vendor invoice can be processed. Invoices and the related general ledger account distribution should be reviewed before recording.

Associated Materials Voucher Sheet (Figure 4-1)

Procedures **Establishment of Control Devices**

4.1 Control should be established over vendor invoices as soon as they are received. Failure to establish control may result in delays in recording the invoice and cause misstatement of accounts payable and the related asset or expense accounts. Furthermore, cash discounts may be lost because of untimely processing. Vendors should be instructed to mail all invoices directly to the accounts payable department (or designated individual in smaller companies). Exceptions to this practice, for items such as confidential services, should be approved, in advance, by a company officer.

Preparation of the Voucher Package

4.2 A voucher sheet (Figure 4-1) should be prepared and a package called the "voucher package" should be assembled with the following documents:

- Vendor invoice.
- Packing slip.
- Purchase order.
- Requisition.
- Receiving report.
- Authorization of acceptance of goods or services. (This may be indicated on the receiving report, purchase order, or memo from the user department.)

Procedures Performed on Voucher Package

4.3 After the voucher package has been assembled (see 4.2) the following procedures should be performed:

- The nature and quantity of goods ordered and the price per the vendor invoice should be compared to the purchase order and the receiving report.
- Calculations of the invoice, such as totals and extensions of quantities multiplied by unit price, should be recomputed.
- The general ledger account distribution should be entered on the voucher sheet. Sometimes an initial account distribution is noted on the purchase order. This procedure is desirable where the requisitioner is more knowledgeable about the general ledger account classification for the related goods or services purchased.
- The voucher package and related general account distribution should be reviewed and approved by a responsible, knowledgeable individual.

  If the company is on a job cost system where purchases of goods and services are for a specific job, the purchase order should contain the job number for the related purchase. The job number should also be listed on the voucher sheet so that the purchases can be charged to the appropriate job.

Processing of Freight Bills

4.4 The company may receive freight bills for goods received from vendors and for goods shipped to customers. The following procedures apply to the processing of freight bills:

(a) Freight bills for goods received usually require the following procedures for processing:

    (1) The bill of lading should be routed from the receiving department to the accounts payable department. If the company determines that the purchasing department should review the shipping terms and amount, the bill of lading should first be routed to the

purchasing department and then to the accounts payable department.

(2) When the invoice for freight is received, the invoice should be matched with the bill of lading and a copy of the related purchase order. The purchase order should contain the following information on the shipping terms:

- Who pays the freight
- Type of transportation
- Carrier, if known
- Cost

(3) A voucher sheet (see 4.2) should be attached to the above documents.

(4) General ledger account distribution should be documented on the voucher sheet. Freight cost that relates to materials and services that become part of the company's product should be assigned to a "cost of sales" general ledger account or an inventory account, depending on the company's method of accounting for inventory.

(5) If the company has a purchase history file, whether manual or computerized, and the costs in this file are used to price the company's inventory, the freight cost per the freight bill should be allocated to the various materials purchased and included in the cost of material in the purchase history file.

(b) Freight bills for shipments to customers are usually processed as follows:

(1) A voucher package should be assembled with the following documents:

- A bill of lading routed from the shipping department.
- Notification that goods were received by the customer, which is usually a copy of the bill of lading signed by the customer.
- Purchase order from the customer that gives terms and price quote for shipment. The price may also be based on according to a master contract.
- Voucher sheet.

(2) A general ledger account should be listed on the voucher. The general ledger account should preferably be labeled as shipping or delivery expense.

Guidelines for C.O.D. Purchases

4.5 Cash on delivery (C.O.D.) purchases should be discouraged. When it becomes necessary for the company to have C.O.D. purchases, a check request form should be prepared, as previously discussed in Section IV—3.0. When the goods are delivered, the following procedures are appropriate:

- The goods should be inspected by the receiving department (3.1).
- The bill of lading, purchase order, and vendor invoice should be immediately stamped "paid."
- The documents should not be sent to the accounts payable department. Instead, they should be sent to the department handling the preparation of checks and the recording of cash disbursements.
- The person responsible for signing checks should review the completed documents to ascertain that the documents are complete and company procedures were followed.

Recording Invoice in the Voucher Register or Purchase Journal

4.6 After the voucher package is complete, the vendor invoice is ready for recording. The following information should be entered into the voucher register or purchase journal. (Voucher register and purchase journal are similar type accounting records. The purchase journal is more commonly used in manual systems.)

- Voucher number
- Vendor name
- Vendor invoice number
- Date of vendor invoice
- Amount of invoice
- General ledger account
- Date invoice is to be paid
- Discount, if applicable

4.6.1 Upon the posting of the vendor invoice to the voucher register or purchase journal, the vendor invoice has been recorded in the accounting system as a liability. Control over the completeness of posting should be provided by batch control totals. The use of control totals can be accomplished by running an adding machine tape of the invoice amounts. The total posted into the voucher register or purchase journal should equal the adding machine tape total.

4.6.2 A similar use of control totals can be accomplished by arithmetically proving that the ending amount of accounts payable is equal to the sum of the beginning balance, plus posted vendor invoice amounts, less cash payments.

Posting Vendor Invoices to the Accounts Payable Subledger

4.7 When vendor invoices are posted to the voucher register or purchases journal, the amount of the invoice should also be posted to the accounts payable subsidiary ledger. The accounts payable subsidiary ledger is a file of the individual vendors and the amount owed to each vendor. Likewise, cash payments to vendors should also be posted to the accounts payable subsidiary ledger. The total of amounts owed to the vendors per the accounts payable subsidiary ledger should equal the accounts payable account total per the general ledger (control account).

Reconciliation of A/P Subledger to A/P General Ledger

4.8   At the end of each accounting period, the total amounts due to vendors per the accounts payable subsidiary ledger should be reconciled to the total per the accounts payable general ledger account (control account). All differences should be investigated and adjustments made as necessary. The reconciliation and the results of investigation of differences should be reviewed and approved by a responsible official.

In addition, the accounts payable subsidiary ledger should be maintained by individuals other than those who post to the accounts payable subsidiary ledger and who maintain the control account in the general ledger.

Review of Debit Balances in Accounts Payable

4.9   The accounts payable subsidiary ledger should be reviewed at least monthly for debit balances (amounts vendors owe to the company). In reviewing debit balances, the designated employee should ascertain if the company will receive cash from the vendor or if an offset to another invoice is appropriate. If there is a significant dollar amount of debit balances in accounts payable, this debit balance should be removed from accounts payable and recorded in accounts receivable.

Reconciliation of A/P Subsidiary Records to Suppliers' Records

4.10   Accounts payable subsidiary records should be periodically reconciled to suppliers' records by comparison with suppliers' statements.

Approval and Review of Discrepancies in 4.10

4.11   The reconciliations in 4.10 and the results of any investigation of differences should be reviewed and approved by a responsible official.

SECTION X
FIGURE 4-1

Voucher Sheet

Voucher Number _____

Vendor Number _____

Invoice Date _____ $ _____

Due Date _____

<u>Gross Amount</u>   <u>Discount</u>

_____

<u>Account No.</u>   <u>Amount</u>

_____

Extensions Checked _____

Columns Footed _____

Purchasing Approval _____

Receiving Report _____

Freight _____

_____

Prepared by   Approved by

5. RETURN OF GOODS TO SUPPLIERS

Policy   Returns of goods to suppliers should be adequately controlled, documented, and recorded.

General   The return of goods to suppliers should be under a controlled system of procedures. These procedures should include the authorization of the return by the requisitioning department or purchasing function, preparation of a debit memorandum by the purchasing department, recording of the debit memorandum, and follow-up with supplier to ascertain that the supplier has recognized the return of goods.

Associated Materials   Materials Rejection Report (Figure 5-1)
Debit Memorandum (Figure 5-2)

Procedures   **Preparation of a Rejection of Material Report**

5.1   Claims for return of goods in many companies are likely to be nonroutine and infrequent. Furthermore, detection of goods to be returned may occur at various stages of a company's operations (i.e., receiving, raw material warehouse, production, finished goods inspection, or returns from customers). The first step should be to have the department detecting the improper goods prepare a materials rejection report (Figure 5-1). This report should contain the following information and authorizations:

(a)   Part number

(b)   Description of part

(c)   Department and person rejecting the part

(d)   Quantity received and rejected

(e)   Reason for rejection

(f)   Purchase order number

(g)   Date received

(h)   Vendor

(i)   Authorization signatures:
- Person in charge of department in which rejected goods are noted
- Operations manager or person who made the requisition, if this authorization is deemed necessary
- Purchasing department

The materials rejection report should be prenumbered so that it can subsequently be established that all transctions have been accounted for.

The purchasing department should be notified immediately about the rejected materials. Typically, the rejected goods should be sent to the shipping department with a copy of the materials rejection report. If the rejection of materials is unique, the department should wait for instructions from the purchasing department regarding disposition of the rejected materials.

Shipment of Goods Back to Vendor

5.2   When the rejected goods are received in the shipping department, the goods should be handled similarly to shipment of the company's finished goods. A bill of lading should be prepared as well as a packing slip (see Section V—2.5). In this situation, the company should consider using a copy of the debit memorandum (see 5.3) as a packing slip. A copy of the packing slip and the bill of lading should be sent to the purchasing department.

Preparation of a Debit Memorandum for Returned Goods

5.3   The debit memorandum (Figure 5-2) is the form that the company uses to record the return of goods to the supplier. The debit memorandum serves as a notification to the supplier that goods are being returned and the company is expecting a credit for the returned items. The debit memorandum should be prepared by the purchasing department. The debit memorandum forms should be sequentially numbered. Before the debit memorandum is prepared, the purchasing department should contact the supplier regarding the return of goods. Such a procedure will alert the supplier to the return of the goods, allow the supplier to react on a timely basis if replacement goods are needed, avoid problems relating to shipping terms and other conditions, and help the supplier determine whether any special instructions need to be followed. The debit memorandum should include the following information:

- Name and address of supplier.
- Specific name of supplier's employee who will handle the debit memorandum, such as the sales representative or manager of customer relations. Notification of a specific individual at the supplier may help in receiving prompt attention for the returned goods.
- Part number and description of goods returned.
- Quantity returned.
- Reason for return.
- Expected amount of credit from supplier.
- If a cash payment from the supplier is desired, this should also be noted.

Circulation of Debit Memo

5.4   Copies of the debit memorandum should be sent to the following:

(a)   Supplier.

(b)   Shipping department (2 copies), if used as a packing slip.

(c)   Purchasing department should retain one copy.

(d)   Accounts payable. Two copies should be sent to the accounts payable department. The first copy should be sent immediately to accounts payable after the memorandum is prepared to alert accounts payable to the returned goods. This allows the accounts payable department to adjust the payments to the supplier and thus avoid paying for goods that have been returned. The first copy should be filed into a ledger of sequentially numbered debit memos that can be used to ascertain that all debit memos have been received and recorded.

The second copy of the debit memo should come from the purchasing department with the bill of lading, copy of the packing slip, and rejection of materials report. After recording the debit memo, the debit memo and related shipping documents should be filed in the supplier's accounts payable file.

Comparison of Original Invoice Price to Debit Memorandum

5.5   Debit memorandum prices should be compared to the original invoice by persons other than the preparers of the internal debit memorandum. In addition, extensions and additions should be checked to an adequate extent.

Review of Materials Rejection Reports

5.6   Periodically, materials rejection reports should be reviewed to ensure that debit memoranda have been prepared for all returned goods. Any differences should be investigated on a timely basis.

Receipt of Credit Memorandum from Vendor

5.7   The vendor will send a credit memorandum to the company acknowledging the receipt of the returned goods and the dollar amount of the credit given to the company. The accounts payable department should compare the credit memorandum to the internally generated debit memorandum. Agreement with the credit memorandum should be documented in the ledger of sequentially numbered debit memos. Differences should be investigated on a timely basis.

Review of Unmatched Credit (Debit) Memorandum

5.8   Periodically, the ledger of sequentially numbered debit memos should be reviewed to see if the credit memorandum has been received from the supplier. Follow-up with the supplier should be made for unmatched debit memos.

Furthermore, the accounts payable subsidiary ledger should be reviewed for debit balances (indicates that the vendor owes money to the company). If payments are expected from the vendor and have not been received on a timely basis, the vendor should be contacted.

Review and Approval of Discrepancies in 5.7 and 5.8

5.9   The results of the procedures in 5.7 and 5.8 and any adjustments to suppliers' accounts should be reviewed and approved by a responsible official.

SECTION X
FIGURE 5-1

Materials Rejection Report

MATERIALS REJECTION REPORT

Responsibility: Supervisor

Name of Vendor ___(H)_____

Description _____(B)_____

Cat/Part # _____(A)_____   Purchase Order # ____(F)_____

Department _____(C)_____   Date Received _____(G)_____

Quantity Received ____(D)_____   Quantity Rejected ____(D)_____

Reason for Rejection ____(E)_____

_____

_____

_____(I)_____
Signature

SECTION X
FIGURE 5-2

Debit Memorandum

XYZ Company   Debit Memo

No.

V
E
N
D
O
R

DATE:

ATT. ACCOUNTS RECEIVABLE

PLEASE FORWARD NEW INVOICE
AT TIME OF RESHIPMENT

THE FOLLOWING MATERIAL DOES NOT CONFORM TO THE DRAWING AND/OR SPECIFICATIONS ON OUR P.O. NO.

P.O. NUMBER	DATE RECEIVED	MRA NO.	AUTHORIZED BY	CREDIT ONLY ☐ DO NOT REPLACE	REPLACEMENT REQUIRED BY	
ITEM	DESCRIPTION OF MATERIAL			PART NO.	QUANTITY REJECTED	PRICE	EXTENSION

REASON FOR REJECTION

6. *PURCHASE CUT-OFF*

Policy   The liability for goods or services should be recorded in the same accounting period in which the goods are received or services are provided.

General   At the end of accounting period, procedures should be in place to ascertain that the related liabilities for goods or services received during the accounting period are also recorded in the same accounting period.

Associated
Materials   None

Procedures   **Procedures for Proper Purchasing Cut-Off at End of Accounting Period**

6.1   Time delays in receiving and processing vendor invoices for goods and services can cause a company to record the liabilities for the related goods and services in a subsequent accounting period. A company should implement special procedures at the end of an accounting period to ascertain that all liabilities are recorded and a proper purchasing cut-off is achieved. These special procedures include the following:

(a)   Closing of the accounting records should be delayed for a few days to allow receipt of vendor invoices.

(b)   Receiving reports should be stamped "before end of period" to indicate that goods or services have been received in the accounting period and that the related liability must be reported. This should be performed for receipts on or shortly before the last day of the accounting period.

(c)   Likewise, receiving reports for goods received shortly after the last day of the accounting period should be stamped "after end of period."

(d)   Receiving reports that have not been matched with the related vendor invoice should be accumulated and a liability recorded. Recording this liability is a special entry because the related invoices have not been processed through the voucher system. The dollar amounts for these liabilities can usually be obtained from the related purchase orders.

(e)   Typically, the entry to record the liability for unmatched receiving reports, as discussed in (d) above, should be reversed in the subsequent accounting period.

(f)   The numerical file of receiving reports kept in the receiving department should be reviewed to ensure that all receiving reports for goods received during the period have been processed through the accounts payable system or included in the purchase cut-off entry for unmatched receiving reports.

Section XI

NOTES PAYABLE AND LONG-TERM DEBT

1. *FINANCIAL RESOURCE REQUIREMENTS*

Policy The company should establish an orderly system for anticipating financial resource requirements and analyzing the most effective means of providing for those needs.

General Debt, in the broadest definition of the term, is the result of borrowing funds for a specific purpose for a specific period of time. It represents one of the two major means of providing financial resources for an enterprise. The other, the issuance of additional capital stock, is discussed in Section XIV.

Short-term financing consists of debt that is expected to be repaid within the normal operating cycle of the business or within one year of the balance sheet date and can take the form of a line of credit agreement with a bank or demand notes payable.

Long-term financing is primarily debt that will not be repaid within the normal operating cycle of the business or within one year. This financing, used for longer-term needs such as capital improvements and business expansion, will take the form of installment loans, mortgages, bonds, debentures, and capital leases.

Associated Materials None

Procedures Corporate financing through the issuance of debt can entail any number of different forms and types of indebtedness. The more common forms of debt follow:

Notes Payable

1.1 Notes payable are primarily used to meet short-term working capital needs. This debt is often collateralized by certain assets such as customer receivables; inventory; or property, plant, and equipment.

1.1.1 Demand notes should usually be classified as a current liability because the repayment date is not specified.

1.1.2 Other notes payable may have a specified repayment date. These notes should be classified as current or noncurrent based on the specified repayment date.

1.1.3 Interest expense must be accrued on all notes payable, whether they are demand notes or not. Interest must be imputed on non-interest-bearing notes or notes with unrealistically low interest rates. Interest should be accrued monthly over the term of the note based upon the balance of the notes payable, the stated (or imputed) interest rate, and the interest payment dates specified on the notes.

Installment and Mortgage Loans

1.2 Installment and mortgage loans are debt instruments used primarily to finance the acquisition of a specific asset. Most frequently, these loans are collateralized by the land, buildings or equipment acquired. The repayment terms of an installment or mortgage loan usually call for periodic payments to be made over the life of the debt. These payments include both an interest and principal portion. The lender should provide the borrower with an amortization schedule showing a breakdown between the interest and principal portion of each payment.

1.2.1 Based upon the amortization schedule, the principal portion of the payments due within the next year should be classified as a current liability while the remaining principal balance should be classified as long term.

1.2.2 Interest expense on installment and mortgage loans should be accrued and paid based on the amortization schedule referred to above.

Bonds

1.3 Corporate bonds, a form of long-term financing more prevalent among larger corporations, is used to finance larger capital projects such as the construction of a new manufacturing facility or to finance a significant business expansion such as the purchase of equipment for a new product line. Often bonds are secured by most of the assets of the company with bond holders having priority over many of the other creditors.

1.3.1 Interest on corporate bonds should be accrued monthly using the specified rate.

1.3.2 Amortization of bond discounts and premiums must also be recorded monthly based upon amortization schedules prepared when the bonds were issued.

1.3.3 Detailed records should be maintained of the periodic deposits into a sinking fund required under some bond agreements.
- The requisite deposits should be made on a timely basis into a separate fund.
- Statements from the fund trustee (usually a bank or trust company) should be reviewed and any discrepancies investigated and resolved.
- Investment income from the fund should be recorded on a timely basis.
- Upon retirement of the bonds, any deficit or surplus in the sinking fund should be transferred from or to the general cash account.

Long-Term Leases

1.4 Long-term capital leasing is another means by which the purchase of equipment can be financed. The terms of a lease agreement usually call for equal periodic payments over the life of the lease. If a lease meets the criteria classification as a capital lease, the present value of the minimum lease payments is considered to be the long-term debt while the remaining portion of the minimum lease payments is considered to be the interest related to this debt.

1.4.1 An amortization schedule should be prepared showing the breakdown of each payment between the principal and interest portions. As with other installment loans, the principal portion of the minimum lease payments due in the next year should be classified as a current liability while the remaining principal balance should be classified as long term.

1.4.2 The interest portion of capital leases should be recorded and paid based on the amortization schedule referred to above.

2. ASSUMPTION AND AUTHORIZATION OF DEBT

Policy Determination of the need to assume debt should be made by company officials, and all debt should be appropriately authorized.

General The issuance of all new debt as well as the extension of any existing debt should be authorized by the board of directors or, in the case of a smaller company, by a responsible official of the company. This authorization should be documented in the minutes of the board of directors meetings in the form of a resolution. In some instances the creditor will require that a board resolution authorizing the debt be included in the executed debt agreements.

Associated Materials None

Procedures **Board of Directors Resolution**

2.1 A resolution of the board of directors should be prepared so as to document the board's approval of the issuance of the debt.

Debt Approval and Agreement

2.2 A copy of the resolution approving the issuance of the debt should be maintained with the executed copy of the debt agreement.

Records and Collateralization of Debt

2.3 A record should be maintained of the assets collateralizing the debt, if any.
  • The assets should be specifically identified.
  • The record should be updated periodically (e.g., depreciation noted) to reflect the current book value of the assets.

Company Name	Date
Approval	

3. SAFEKEEPING OF DEBT AGREEMENTS

Policy   Physical control of debt instruments should be maintained.

General   The original executed debt agreements and debt instruments should be maintained in a safe place and the existence of these instruments should be verified periodically.

Associated
Materials   None

Procedures   **Original Agreements and Instruments**

     3.1   The original debt agreements and instruments should be obtained once they have been executed.

Physical Safety of Agreements and Instruments

     3.2   These debt agreements and instruments, as well as any subsequent amendments, should be kept in a safe place such as a vault or a safety deposit box. Consideration may be given to having these agreements and instruments maintained by the company's legal counsel at an outside location.

```
┌─────────────────────────────────────────────────────────────────┐
│  ─────────────────────────────────        ─────────────────      │
│  Company Name                              Date                   │
│  ─────────────────────────────                                    │
│  Approval                                                         │
└─────────────────────────────────────────────────────────────────┘
```

4. *RECORD OF DEBT*

Policy   All debt should be recorded in the general ledger based on the terms of the debt agreements.

General   The issuance of any new debt or the extension of any existing debt should be accurately recorded in the general ledger based on the terms of the debt agreement that has been reviewed and approved by the board of directors.

Associated Materials   None

Procedures   **Cash Received in Exchange for Debt**

4.1   When cash received in exchange for certain debt, such as notes payable and bonds, is included in the standard cash receipts system, the entry to initially record this debt is prepared as part of the cash receipts process described earlier. It is, however, important to properly identify the offsetting credit (i.e., notes payable, bank, bonds payable, etc.) and classify the debt as current or long term based upon the repayment terms.

Cash received in exchange for debt may be received via bank wire transfer or some other infrequently used method. In these instances it will be necessary to prepare and record a general journal entry.

(a)   The main objectives, however, of identifying the offsetting credit and of classifying the debt as current or long term remain significant.

(b)   If these journal entries are prepared as part of the standard cash receipts process, a supervisory review is necessary to ensure that the offsetting credit is properly identified and the debt is properly classified between current and long term.

Property, Plant, and Equipment in Exchange for Debt

4.2   Property, plant, and equipment can be received in exchange for installment loans, mortgages, and capital leases. The controls over the cash receipts system, however, cannot be relied upon to identify new debt.

(a) A general journal entry must be prepared to properly record the issuance of this debt and the corresponding property, plant, or equipment.

(b) For installment loans and mortgages, the principal portion of the debt plus any down payment made will equal the cost of the property, plant, and equipment acquired.

(c) For capital leases, the cost of the equipment will be the present value of the minimum lease payments plus any down payment paid.

(d) A supervisory review of the journal entry and the supporting documentation should be performed to ensure the appropriateness and accuracy of the entry.

Bond Price Fluctuations

4.3 Bond prices will fluctuate when the interest rate specified on the bonds differs from the prevailing market interest rates.

(a) A discount or premium is recorded for the difference between the face value of the bonds and the issuance price.

(b) The discount or premium should be amortized over the term of the bonds.

```
┌─────────────────────────────────────────────────────────────┐
│  _____          _____     │
│  Company Name                      Date                       │
│                                                               │
│  _____                                     │
│  Approval                                                     │
└─────────────────────────────────────────────────────────────┘
```

5. *TIMELY INTEREST EXPENSE ACCRUALS*

Policy   Interest expense for all debt should be accrued on a timely basis.

General   An interest accrual should be recorded at the end of each month for all debt on the general ledger.

Associated Materials   None

Procedures   **Interest Accrual Using Amortization Schedule**

5.1   When an amortization schedule is available, the interest accrual should be computed based upon the interest portion of the next payment due and the number of days from the date of the previous payment until the end of the period.

Interest Accrual with Amortization Schedule

5.2   In situations where an amortization schedule is not available, the interest accrual must be computed based upon the principal outstanding during the period, the interest rate charged or imputed by the creditor, and the period of time from the date of the last interest payment until the end of the month.

6. *DEBT PAYMENTS*

Policy All payments should be properly recorded in the general ledger on a timely basis.

General Payment on notes payable and other long-term debt made through the company's standard disbursements system, through the transfer of funds by wire or other method should be recorded on a timely basis.

Associated Materials None

Procedures **Separate Principal and Interest Components**

6.1 For debt that combines both principal and interest into one payment, it is necessary to record the separate principal and interest components of each payment.

(a) If an amortization schedule is to be provided by the creditor, it should be obtained when the debt agreements are executed or as soon thereafter as possible.

(b) If an amortization schedule is not provided, it should be prepared based on the terms of the debt agreement.

(c) A copy of the amortization schedule should be maintained with the original executed debt agreements. A copy should also be sent to the accounting department so that each periodic payment can be properly recorded in the general ledger.

Debt Payment Through General Ledger Distribution

6.2 If the debt payment is made through the company's standard disbursement system, reliance should be placed on the general ledger account distribution process. The account distribution coding for these payments should be reviewed to ensure that the notes payable or other long-term debt and the related interest accrual are properly relieved in accordance with the applicable amortization schedule and other supporting documents.

Debt Payment by Other Method

6.3 Payments made by wire transfer or other method should be recorded through a general journal entry. The general journal entry account distribution for each payment should be supported by the related amortization schedule and other documentation.

7. BOND DISCOUNTS AND PREMIUMS

Policy Bond discounts and premiums should be amortized over the term of the bonds.

General Bonds normally may be issued for a price that differs from the face or maturity value of the bonds. This difference will be either a premium if the sales price is in excess of the face value of the bonds or a discount if the sales price is less than the face value of the bonds. The difference must be amortized over the term of the bonds. The method used to compute the amortization is the interest method. The amortization of a premium will reduce the interest expense while the amortization of a discount will increase the interest expense.

Associated Materials None

Procedures **Bond Amortization Schedule**

7.1 A bond amortization schedule utilizing the interest method should be prepared to determine the periodic amortization and the adjustments to the bond carrying value.

Timely Recording of Discounts and Premiums

7.2 The amortization of bond discounts and premiums should be recorded monthly or, at a minimum, when interest is paid.

Company Name	Date
Approval	

8. *CURRENT AND LONG-TERM DEBT SUMMARY*

Policy A detailed summary of current and long-term debt, accrued interest payable, and interest expense should be prepared and reconciled to the general ledger.

General To ensure that all debt activity is being properly recorded on a timely basis, a detailed summary of current and long-term debt balances, accrued interest payable, and interest expense should be prepared periodically and reconciled to the general ledger. This detailed summary should be prepared from amortization schedules, statements from creditors, and internally prepared schedules of debt activity.

Associated Materials None

Procedures **Debt Instrument Activity Summary**

8.1 A summary of activity for each debt instrument should be prepared. This summary should include the balance of the debt at the beginning of the period, plus any new debt issued during the period, less any principal payments made during the period; the activity in the accrued interest payable accounts including the balance at the beginning of the period, plus any additional interest accrued during the period, less any interest paid during the period; and a breakdown of the current and long-term portions of the balance of the debt at the end of the period.

Comparison to General Ledger

8.2 The outstanding debt, accrued interest payable, and interest expense accrued as summarized in the schedule prepared above should then be compared to the general ledger. Any discrepancies among the amounts taken from the summary and the amounts recorded in the general ledger should be investigated and resolved.

Current Portion of Long-Term Debt

8.3   Finally, the current portion of the debt as summarized above should be compared to the amount recorded on the general ledger. If necessary, a journal entry should be recorded to adjust the current portion of long-term debt to agree with the summary schedule.

9. *DEBT COVENANTS*

Policy   All debt covenants should be reviewed periodically.

General   In the event that there is a lack of compliance with restrictive debt covenants, a creditor could deem the borrower to be in default of the debt agreement. This in turn could give the creditor cause to demand immediate repayment of the debt. With this in mind, the debt covenants should be reviewed annually (or more frequently as the covenants require) so as to determine whether all covenant restrictions have been met. If noncompliance is detected, discussions should begin immediately with the bank or other financial institution in order to avoid foreclosure or recall of the debt.

Associated Materials   None

Procedures   **Debt Covenant Review Checklist**

9.1   The debt covenant section of each debt agreement should be reviewed and a separate "debt covenant review checklist" should be prepared for each debt agreement. This checklist should cover all covenants including those requiring the maintenance of certain financial ratios, those requiring the reporting of certain financial information to the bank on a periodic basis, and those limiting the amount of certain expenditures such as capital improvements and dividends. These checklists should be prepared in a format that will provide sufficient space for the calculation of each ratio and that can be carried forward for use in subsequent periods.

Frequency of Checklist Preparation

9.2   Annually, or more frequently if necessary, the checklists prepared above should be completed. All covenants should be reviewed and all required financial ratios should be calculated. A notation should be made on the checklist next to each individual covenant documenting whether or not the company is in compliance with that covenant.

Noncompliance with Debt Covenants

9.3   If noncompliance with certain covenants is noted, communications with the bank or other creditor should be instituted. It may also be necessary to obtain a waiver of the debt covenants from the bank. If such waiver cannot be obtained, it will be necessary to classify the related debt as current.

Section XII

ACCRUED LIABILITIES

Company Name	Date
Approval	

1. *MONITORING OF ACCRUED LIABILITIES*

Policy   The company should establish a method of monitoring and accounting for accrued liabilities.

General   Accrued liabilities, often referred to as accrued expenses or, more simply, accruals, are items for which a service or benefit has been received and for which the related liabilities are both acknowledged and reasonably determinable, but which are not yet payable, either because of the terms of the commitments or because invoices have not yet been received.

Associated
Materials   None

Procedures   **Establishing List of Expenses**

1.1   The accounting department should establish a list of commonly incurred expenses that may have to be accrued at the end of an accounting period. This list will serve as a reminder and help ensure that all expenses have been identified. Examples of such expenses are
- Salaries and wages
- Payroll taxes
- Vacation and sick pay
- Deferred compensation
- Commissions
- Professional fees
- Royalties
- Rent
- Property taxes
- Insurance

- Interest
- Warranty costs

Preparation of Detailed Register

1.2   Once identified, each expense should be maintained in a detailed register (see Section VII—Figure 1-1).

When and How Accrued Liabilities Occur

1.3   The amount recorded for accrued expenses should be properly measured. For example:

- A company pays its employees weekly, and the first pay check of the new year includes salaries and wages for three days in the current year and two days in the subsequent year. In this case, the company would record a journal entry at the end of the year to accrue three-fifths of the weekly payroll amount.

Accrued liabilities come into existence with the passage of time or with the occurrence of an event.

(a)   Most accrued liabilities occur with the passage of time. Examples of these include interest, rent, and property taxes.

(b)   Some accrued liabilities occur with the occurrence of an event, such as a service being performed. Examples of these include payrolls, royalties, sales commissions, and payroll taxes.

Recording the Accrual

1.4   The accounting clerk should prepare a journal entry to record the accrued liability and the matching expense. The preparer should sign or initial the journal entry. The entry should be reviewed and approved by the accounting supervisor and initialed.

Review of the Account Balance

1.5   At the end of each accounting period, a responsible official should review the adequacy of accrued expenses. If any adjustments are deemed appropriate to the account balance, a journal entry should be made to adjust both the accrued expenses and accrued liabilities. This should be reviewed as in 1.4.

2. *RECONCILIATIONS AND ACCURACY*

Policy   Detailed records of accrued liabilities should be reconciled regularly with the control account.

General   Reconciliations should be performed to help ensure the accuracy of the detailed records and the control account.

Associated Materials   None

Procedures   **Performance of Monthly Reconciliations**

2.1   A reconciliation should be performed between the detailed register and the general ledger balance every month. The person performing the reconciliation should not be one who maintains the detailed records and the control account.

Investigation of Discrepancies

2.2   All discrepancies should be investigated on a timely basis.

Supervisory Review of the Reconciliation

2.3   The reconciliation should be reviewed and approved by a responsible official such as the accounting manager. The review should be evidenced by a signature.

Section XIII

PAYROLL CYCLE

Company Name	Date
Approval	

1. *PAYROLL AND PERSONNEL/ HUMAN RESOURCES*

Policy   A system of authorized communication between the payroll and the personnel/human resources departments should be established and maintained.

General   The personnel department maintains employee files in which employee pay history is documented and withholding authorizations are retained. Changes to standing payroll data (see 2.0), which is processed by the payroll department, are generally initiated by the personnel/human resources department (e.g., hiring of new employees, authorization for pay rate increases, etc.).

Associated Materials   None

Procedures   **New Employees**

1.1   A policy should be established by the personnel department regarding the source of new employees. Such a policy may include filling openings by promoting from within the company, with recruitment from outside sources as a second choice. Additionally, policies should be established regarding job postings, recruiting methods, reference checks, compliance with Equal Employment Opportunity requirements, and so on.

1.2   A policy should be established by the personnel department regarding the approvals necessary for the hiring of a new employee. This approval should include the employee's rate of compensation and effective date. This may be reported on a "personnel action form" and forwarded to the payroll department (see 2.0).

Compensation and Evaluation

1.3 Policies should be established relative to periodic evaluation and the determination of increases in compensation.

1.4 A policy should be established regarding the approvals necessary for pay rate changes. This approval should be in writing and by persons independent of the payroll function. These changes and approvals should be reported on a status report and forwarded to the payroll department (see 2.0).

Vacation and Sick Pay

1.5 A policy should be established regarding employees' eligibility for vacation and sick time, including the amount of vacation and sick time pay earned; the period of time in which vacation and sick time can be used; and whether vacation or sick time can be accumulated and for how long.

1.6 Detailed records should be maintained for each employee indicating the vacation and sick time available and utilized.

1.7 No vacation or sick time should be paid until the detailed records are reviewed for propriety of such payment. This check may be incorporated into the payroll software for computerized systems.

Company Name	Date
Approval	

2. *WAGES AND SALARIES*

Policy Payment for wages and salaries should be made only to company employees at authorized rates of pay.

General Controls should be established over standing payroll data to ensure that the payroll reflects complete and authorized standing data.

Associated Materials Personnel Action Form (Figure 2-1)

Procedures **Changes in Payroll Data**

2.1 All changes to standing payroll data should be authorized in writing (Figure 2-1) including:
- New hires
- Terminations
- Pay rate changes
- Voluntary payroll deductions
- Court-ordered payroll deductions

Authorization of Changes in Payroll Data

2.2 Changes to payroll standing data should be authorized by an appropriate official outside of the payroll department.

2.2.1 New hires/terminations should be authorized in writing by the appropriate operating department and the personnel department.

2.2.2 Voluntary deductions should be authorized by the individual employee.

2.2.3 Pay rate changes should be authorized in writing by the personnel department or the appropriate department head.

2.2.4 A copy of all authorization forms for changes to standing payroll data should be retained in each employee's personnel file.

Comparison of Payroll Data to Personnel Files

2.3 The personnel or internal audit department should periodically compare payroll data to the personnel files to ensure that all changes have been made accurately and timely and that only authorized changes have been made.

SECTION XIII
FIGURE 2-1

XYZ Company
Personnel Action Form

DATED _____

NAME _____ SEX ☐ ☐ DATE OF HIRE _____ EMPLOYEE NO. _____
                                    M F

ADDRESS _____ SOC. SEC. NO. _____

CITY _____ HOME PHONE NO. (____) _____

DEPARTMENT _____ JOB TITLE _____

                                            ☐ WAGE   PRESENT _____ /HR
                                            ☐ SALARY RATE _____ /WEEK

TYPE OF CHANGE

☐ NEW HIRE   ☐ RESIGNATION   ☐ RATE CHANGE
☐ REHIRE   ☐ DISCHARGE   ☐ JOB CHANGE
☐ RETURN FROM   ☐ LEAVE OF   ☐ DEPT. CHANGE
  LEAVE   ABSENCE
☐ OTHER

CHANGED TO

☐ WAGE   RATE _____ /HR.
☐ SALARY _____ /WEEK

JOB TITLE _____
DEPARTMENT _____   } EFFECTIVE _____
OTHER _____

REASON FOR CHANGE _____

REMARKS _____

INITIATED BY _____
APPROVED BY _____
PERSONNEL _____

TOOLS AND STORES CLEARED ☐ BY _____   __ / __ / __
ID BADGE RETURNED ☐ BY _____   __ / __ / __
ELIGIBLE FOR REHIRE _____

3. *TIMEKEEPING*

Policy Payment for wages and salaries should be made in accordance with records of work performed.

General Controls should be established over the transaction data (time records, output records) to ensure that disbursements of company funds are for valid services performed.

Associated Materials Time Card (Figure 3-1)
Time Sheet (Figure 3-2)

Procedures **Maintenance of Time Records**

3.1 For employees compensated on the basis of time worked or output, time records (Figures 3-1 and 3-2) and output records should be maintained and approved by department supervisors.

Overtime Approval

3.2 All overtime should be approved by department supervisors.

Reconciliation of Payroll to Supporting Records

3.3 A reconciliation should be performed on transaction data (time worked, output, sales) that is the basis of the payroll calculation to supporting records. Examples are

(a) Batch total of hours from clock cards should be established before the payroll is prepared, then compared to the payroll.

(b) Reported output per employee should be totaled and compared with "production" quantities indicated on records maintained by the cost accounting (or inventory) department.

(c)   For commissioned salesmen, reported sales should be totaled and reconciled with operating sales data.

SECTION XIII
FIGURE 3-1

XYZ Company
Time Card

XYZ Company
Time Card

DEPT.   EMP. NO.

_____   _____

FROM _____   TO _____

SIGNED _____

SAT	SUN	MON	TUES	WED	THURS	FRI

XYZ Company
Time Sheet

XYZ Company
Time Sheet

NAME		SIGNED		
FROM		TO		

JOB #	SAT	MON	TUES	WED	THURS	FRI	TOTAL HOURS
INDIRECT							
OFFICE							
SICKNESS HOLIDAY							
TOTAL HOURS							
SUPPER ALLOWANCE							

NOTES   SEE OVER ☐

1. ENTER HOURS WORKED IN 1/4 HOUR INCREMENTS.
2. THE TOTAL WORK HOURS SHOWN HERE AS WORKED EACH DAY MUST EQUAL THE TOTAL HOURS ACTUALLY
   WORKED EACH DAY WITH DUE REGARD FOR OVERTIME, LATENESS, TIME OFF, ETC.
3. SIGNED TIME SHEETS MUST BE SUBMITTED NOT LATER THAN 5:15 P.M. FRIDAY AFTERNOON

APPD _____

Company Name	Date
Approval	

4. *PAYROLL CALCULATION*

Policy   Payments for wages and salaries should be accurately calculated.

General   Controls should be established to ensure that the payroll, based on standing and transaction data, is accurately calculated.

Associated Materials   None

Procedures   **Time Cards**

4.1   Time clock card details should be summarized by the timekeeping department before payroll preparation. This total should then be compared to the actual payroll.

Payroll Compared to Control Totals

4.2   Gross pay and payroll deductions should be compared to an adequate extent with predetermined control totals by an employee outside of the payroll department. This review should be evidenced in writing.

Independent Payroll Calculations

4.3   Calculations and additions of payrolls and payroll summaries should be checked by an employee outside of the payroll department. This review should be evidenced in writing.

Payroll Authorization

4.4   Payrolls should be subject to final written approval by the controller or other financial official before being paid.

```
┌─────────────────────────────────────────────────────────┐
│  ─────────────────────────────          ──────────────   │
│  Company Name                           Date              │
│                                                           │
│  ─────────────────────────────                           │
│  Approval                                                 │
└─────────────────────────────────────────────────────────┘
```

5. *PAYMENT TO COMPANY EMPLOYEES*

Policy Payment for wages and salaries should be made only to company employees.

General Controls should be established to ensure that only valid company employees receive payroll payments.

Associated Materials None

Procedures **Distribution of Payroll**

5.1 Payroll payments (by cash or check) should be distributed by individuals who do not approve time reports, are not responsible for hiring/firing, and do not control the preparation of the payroll.

Receipt Log for Cash Payments

5.2 If payment is in cash, employees should be required to sign a receipt log.

Comparison of Employee Check Endorsements to Signatures on File

5.3 Periodically, endorsements on checks or signatures on the cash receipt log should be compared with employee signatures on file.

Unclaimed Payroll Checks

5.4 Unclaimed payroll (checks or cash) should be reported and returned to the accounting department. Subsequent payment should require the presentation of appropriate evidence of employment by the employee.

Reconciliation of Payroll Bank Accounts

5.5 The payroll bank account should be reconciled monthly by an employee who has no responsibilities for the preparation of the payroll or physical distribution of paychecks.

```
┌─────────────────────────────────────────────────────────────────┐
│  _____        _____     │
│  Company Name            ·                    Date               │
│  _____                               │
│  Approval                                                        │
└─────────────────────────────────────────────────────────────────┘
```

6. *PAYROLL DEDUCTIONS*

Policy Payroll deductions should be correctly recorded and paid to the appropriate third parties on a timely basis. Also, related payroll reports to third parties should be submitted on a timely basis.

General Controls should be established to ensure that payroll deductions, both compulsory and voluntary, are adequately identifiable in the general ledger and that the payments to the third parties are timely and accurate.

Associated Materials None

Procedures **Recording of Payroll Deductions**

6.1   Payroll deductions should be recorded in separate general ledger control accounts.

Independent Check of Payroll Deductions

6.2   Payments of payroll deductions to third parties should be reconciled with the related payrolls by an employee outside of the payroll department.

Review of Payroll Deductions Payments to Third Parties

6.3   Payments of payroll deductions to third parties, including the employer payroll expense portion where applicable, and the related documentation should be reviewed by a financial official to ensure that payments are appropriate and made on a timely basis.

CAPITAL STOCK

```
┌─────────────────────────────────────────────────────────────┐
│  _____        _____ │
│  Company Name                             Date                │
│  _____                            │
│  Approval                                                     │
└─────────────────────────────────────────────────────────────┘
```

1. *AUTHORIZATION, ISSUANCE, AND MAINTENANCE OF CAPITAL STOCK*

Policy Adequate controls should be maintained over sales and issuances of capital stock.

General All capital transactions should be recorded in accordance with the prescribed accounting principles for the type of entity and appropriate legal guidelines (e.g., state laws, articles of incorporation, partnership agreement, etc.).

Associated Materials None

Procedures **Approval by Board of Directors**

1.1 The initial issuance and sale of stock, and subsequent issuances of stock, should be approved by the board of directors. The approval is to be documented in writing (i.e., board minutes) and should identify all relevant terms including:
- Number of shares
- Price per share
- Conditions to be satisfied before issuance

Issuance of Certificates

1.2 Stock certificates should be issued only upon written evidence that the required consideration for the shares has been received by the corporation.

Stock certificates should be sequentially numbered and should identify:

- Name of the corporation
- Signature of corporate official
- Holder's name
- Number of shares represented by the certificate
- Class and type of stock (common or preferred)
- Date issued

Transferability of Stock Certificates

1.3 When a stockholder transfers all or a portion of his or her shares to another party, the original certificate should be canceled and a new certificate issued upon receipt by the corporation of a stock assignment form signed by the original stockholder. Surrendered certificates should be retained with the corporate stock records.

Maintaining Permanent Evidence of Transfer

1.4 A receipt or equivalent evidence of transfer should be provided by the stockholder and retained with the corporate stock records.

Issuance of Stock When Full Payment Is Received

1.5 Subscribed stock should not be issued until the consideration is received in full. The subscription agreement, including specific repayment terms, will be evidenced in writing.

```
┌─────────────────────────────────────────────────────────────┐
│  ─────────────────────────────────      ──────────────────   │
│  Company Name                            Date                 │
│                                                               │
│  ─────────────────────────────────                           │
│  Approval                                                     │
└─────────────────────────────────────────────────────────────┘
```

2. *OUTSTANDING STOCK PROCEDURES*

Policy Appropriate records of outstanding capital stock should be maintained.

General Complete and accurate records should be maintained in order to provide accountability for all transactions.

Associated Materials None

Procedures **Maintenance of Stock Journal**

2.1   The company should maintain a stock journal (or stock register) for each class and type of stock issued. Such journal should include:

- Certificate number
- Date of purchase
- Holder's name and address
- Number of shares
- Par value
- Additional paid in capital
- Description of any rights, provisions, or restrictions

For stock that has been subscribed, the journal should also include:
- Amount subscribed
- Date and amount of payments
- Remaining balance receivable

Preparation of Registrar Reports

2.2   In cases where the company employs a transfer agent and registrar, the company should obtain reports from the registrar containing activity for the period. Periodically, an appropriate official should reconcile the activity as reported by the transfer agent and the registrar to capital stock transactions authorized by the company.

Posting to the General Ledger Accounts

2.3   Totals from the subsidiary records should be posted to the appropriate general ledger accounts (for each class and type of stock):

- Par value
- Additional paid in capital
- Subscription receivable
- Capital stock subscribed

All journal entries should be reviewed and approved by a responsible official.

3. CAPITAL STOCK RECORDS

Policy Detailed capital stock records should be reconciled regularly with the control account.

General Reconciliations should be performed to help ensure the accuracy of the detailed records and the control account.

Associated Materials None

Procedures: **Reconciliation to General Ledger**

   3.1 A reconciliation should be performed on a regular basis between the stock journal (or register) and the general ledger control account. The person performing the reconciliation should be one other than those who:

   (a) maintain the detailed records;

   (b) maintain the control account;

   (c) are responsible for cash functions;

   (d) are responsible for custody of unissued stock certificates.

   Examination of Unissued and Retired Stock Certificates

   3.2 As part of the reconciliation process, an examination should be made of all the unissued and retired stock certificates, and it should be compared to the detailed records.

   Investigation of Discrepancies

   3.3 All discrepancies should be investigated on a timely basis.

   Approval of Reconciliation, Examination, and Investigation

   3.4 The reconciliation and the results thereof should be reviewed and approved by a responsible official.

PART II

FULL-SIZED FORMS

This section contains full-sized versions of all the forms referenced, illustrated, and explained in the procedures presented in Part I. The reference letters that were used for instruction purposes in the procedures have been removed from these versions. The forms are ready to be modified, if required, and identified with a company name and/or logo, then reproduced. The figure in parentheses in the following Index of Forms references the section in Part I where the form is discussed.

INDEX OF FORMS

1. Service Request Form (Section II—Figure 3-1)
2. Cataloging Authorization Form (Section II—Figure 3-2)
3. Operations Schedule (Section II—Figure 4-1)
4. Operator Incident Log (Section II—Figure 4-2)
5. Access Request Form (Section II—Figure 5-1)
6. Journal Voucher (Section III—Figure 2-1)
7. Check Request Form (Section IV—Figure 3-1)
8. Check Control Log (Section IV—Figure 3-2)
9. Bank Reconciliation (Section IV—Figure 5-1)
10. Sales Order Form (Section V—Figure 2-1)
11. Shipping Log (Section V—Figure 2-2)
12. Sales Invoice (Section V—Figure 3-1)
13. Credit Memo (Section V—Figure 5-1)
14. Materials Requisition Form (Section VI—Figure 3-1)
15. Inventory Tag (Section VI—Figure 5-1)
16. Investment Control Log (Section VIII—Figure 1-1A, 1-1B)
17. Investment Purchase/Sale Authorization Form (Section VIII—Figure 1-2)
18. Investment Gain/Loss Calculation Worksheet (Section VIII—Figure 1-3)
19. Safekeeping Receipt Form (Section VIII—Figure 2-1)
20. Interest Income Worksheet (Section VIII—Figure 3-1)
21. Dividend Earnings Worksheet (Section VIII—Figure 3-2)
22. Appropriations Request Form (Section IX—Figure 1-1)
23. Detailed Fixed Asset Ledger (Section IX—Figure 2-1)
24. Disposal Form (Section IX—Figure 5-1)
25. Requisition Form (Section X—Figure 1-1)
26. Approval Limit Schedule (Section X—Figure 2-1)
27. Purchase Order (Section X—Figure 2-2)
28. Receiving Report—Description and Quantity Manually Written (Section X—Figure 3-1)
29. Receiving Report—Copy of Purchase Order Used (Section X—Figure 3-2)
30. Receiving Control Log (Section X—Figure 3-3)
31. Voucher Sheet (Section X—Figure 4-1)
32. Materials Rejection Report (Section X—Figure 5-1)
33. Debit Memorandum (Section X—Figure 5-2)
34. Personnel Action Form (Section XIII—Figure 2-1)
35. Time Card (Section XIII—Figure 3-1)
36. Time Sheet (Section XIII—Figure 3-2)

Service Request Form

PART I (Completed by Requesting Department)

Service Request Description _____
_____
_____
_____

Expected Benefits _____
_____
_____
_____

PART II

User Department: Requested by _____ Date _____

Approved by _____ Date _____

Data Processing: Approved by _____ Date _____

Data Processing Use Only

SRF No. _____

Estimated Effort _____

SRF Disposition _____
_____

Cataloging Authorization Form

PART I   (Completed by Programmer)

Program Name _____

Library Name _____

Modification Description _____

_____

_____

Target Implementation Date_____

PART II   (Completed by Reviewer)

Job Control Statements Reviewed _____

Documentation Updated and Reviewed _____

Operations Procedures Updated and Reviewed _____

Test Results Reviewed_____

PART III

User Department: Requested by _____ Date _____

                    Approved by _____ Date _____

Data Processing: Approved by _____ Date _____

```
┌─────────────────────────────────────────────────────────────┐
│                   Data Processing Use Only                    │
│                                                               │
│   Implemented (Date) _____   │
│                                                               │
│   Signed _____    │
│                                                               │
└─────────────────────────────────────────────────────────────┘
```

Operations Schedule

Date_____   Day _____

Daily Jobs	(1)	(2)	Weekly Jobs	(1)	(2)	Periodic Jobs	(1)	(2)
_____	—	—	_____	—	—	_____	—	—
_____	—	—	_____	—	—	_____	—	—
_____	—	—	_____	—	—	_____	—	—
_____	—	—	_____	—	—	_____	—	—
_____	—	—	_____	—	—	_____	—	—
_____	—	—	_____	—	—	_____	—	—
_____	—	—	_____	—	—	_____	—	—
_____	—	—	_____	—	—	_____	—	—
_____	—	—	_____	—	—	_____	—	—
_____	—	—	_____	—	—	_____	—	—
_____	—	—	_____	—	—	_____	—	—
_____	—	—	_____	—	—	_____	—	—
_____	—	—	_____	—	—	_____	—	—
_____	—	—	_____	—	—	_____	—	—
_____	—	—	_____	—	—	_____	—	—
_____	—	—	_____	—	—	_____	—	—
_____	—	—	_____	—	—	_____	—	—
_____	—	—	_____	—	—	_____	—	—
_____	—	—	_____	—	—	_____	—	—
_____	—	—	_____	—	—	_____	—	—
_____	—	—	_____	—	—	_____	—	—
_____	—	—	_____	—	—	_____	—	—
_____	—	—	_____	—	—	_____	—	—

(1) Check off when job is completed.

(2) Note any error/amend codes. Refer to incident log for disposition.

Operator Incident Log

Date	Time	Description of Trouble	Disposition/Explanation
_____	_____	_____	_____
_____	_____	_____	_____
_____	_____	_____	_____
_____	_____	_____	_____
_____	_____	_____	_____
_____	_____	_____	_____
_____	_____	_____	_____
_____	_____	_____	_____
_____	_____	_____	_____
_____	_____	_____	_____
_____	_____	_____	_____

Access Request Form

PART I   (Completed by Requesting Department)

Name _____   Tel Extension_____

Department_____   Location _____

Functional Description _____

Specify Access Required _____

_____

_____

_____

If other user in department has identical access needs, give name_____

PART II

User Department: Approved by _____   Date _____

Data Processing: Approved by _____   Date _____

Data Processing Use Only

Entered by _____   Date_____

Verified _____

Menu Name _____

Journal Voucher

_____ Company   Date _____

                                                  Number _____

Account Name	Account Code	Debit	Account Name	Account Code	Credit

Explanation:

_____

Prepared by _____   Date _____

Approved by _____   Date _____

Check Request Form

CHECK REQUEST   No. 501

TO: ACCOUNTING DEPARTMENT

Please issue check payable to:

Name _____   Date _____

Street _____   Amount $ _____

City_____

Purpose _____
_____
_____

Charge to _____

Instructions: Mail to Payee _____

                   Deliver to _____   _____
                                                                        Authorized Signature

Check Control Log

Date	Checks Issued	Issued to	Approved	Returned	Voided	Returned	Approved

Bank Reconciliation

Month _____

A/C # _____

Balance per Bank $

Less Outstanding Checks

Add Deposits in Transit

Other Adjustments

Balance per General Ledger $ _____

_____
Prepared by   Date

_____
Reviewed by   Date

Sales Order Form

_____ COMPANY

SALES ORDER NO.	CUSTOMER ORDER NO.	CUSTOMER DATE	PAGE OF	SALES ORDER DATE

CHARGE TO

TERMS

F.O.B.

REQUIRED ROUTING	Collect	Prepaid	CUSTOMER NO.

PRODUCT CODE	ITEM NO.	Original Qty. Ordered	PART NUMBER	DESCRIPTION	SHIPPING SCHEDULE	UNIT PRICE

SPECIAL INSTRUCTIONS AND MARKS

SALES TAX

%

PACKAGING REQUIREMENTS	COMMERCIAL OTHER	APPROVAL

ORDER BILLING MASTER

Shipping Log

_____ COMPANY

Customer	Shipping Information	Sales Order Number	Shipping Date

Sales Invoice Form

_____ COMPANY

SALES ORDER NO.	CUSTOMER ORDER NO.	CUSTOMER DATE	PAGE OF	SALES ORDER DATE	INVOICE NUMBER	INVOICE DATE

C
H
A
R
G
E

T
O

			TERMS	SHIPMENT DATE	SHIPPED VIA
			F.O.B.	WAYBILL NUMBER	
				NO. OF PACKAGES	

REQUIRED ROUTING		Collect	Prepaid	CUSTOMER NO.	SHIPMENT NUMBER	Partial	Complete	WEIGHT	TERMS CODE

PRODUCT CODE	ITEM NO.	Original Qty. Ordered	PART NUMBER	DESCRIPTION	SHIPPING SCHEDULE	UNIT PRICE	QUANTITY ON BALANCE	QUANTITY THIS SHIPMENT	TOTAL AMOUNT

SPECIAL INSTRUCTIONS AND MARKS

Work Order #

| | TOTAL | |

PACKAGING REQUIREMENTS	COMMERCIAL	OTHER	SALES TAX	%	SALES TAX

APPROVAL

FREIGHT

PAY THIS AMOUNT ➡

266 / *PART II*

Credit Memorandum

No.

VENDOR NO. _____

DATE _____

P.O. NO. _____

CHARGE _____

ATTN: ACCOUNTS PAYABLE

REF. INV. NO. _____

ITEM	DESCRIPTION	PART NO.	QUANTITY	UNIT PRICE	AMOUNT

Authorized Signature   Date

Materials Requisition Form

Company Requisition

UNIT NO. _____   JOB NO. _____   DATE _____
PAGE _____ OF _____

C O D E	PART NUMBER	PART DESCRIPTION	QUANTITY				UNIT COST	TOTAL COST
			REQ'D	ISSUED	RETURNED	B/O		

TOTAL =

ISSUED BY _____   RECEIVED BY _____   DATE ISSUED _____

APPROVED BY _____

Inventory Tag

Tag # _____

Location: Area _____
            Row _____
            Column _____

Type: RM _____
       FG _____
       WIP _____

Qty _____

Unit of Measure _____

Description _____

Inventory Coding _____

Remarks _____

Counted by _____

Checked by _____

Investment Control Log

Purchases

Investment Number	Description	Authorization Date	Amount	Broker/ Agent	Trade Date	Settlement Date

Investment Control Log

Sales

Investment Number	Description	Authorization Date	Amount	Broker/ Agent	Trade Date	Settlement Date

Number _____

Investment Purchase/Sale Authorization Form

Date _____ Investment number _____

Investment Type _____

Investment Description _____

Amount: Purchase _____

           Sale _____

Expected Trade Date _____

Expected Settlement Date _____

Broker/Agent _____

Commission _____

Other Expenses _____

Safekeeping Arrangements _____

_____

_____

_____

	Signature	Title	Date
Preparer	_____	_____	_____
Authorization	_____	_____	_____

Three copies of this form should be prepared, with distribution as follows:

     original—investment file
     copy #1—attached to check request
     copy #2—retained by preparer
     copy #3—numerical sequence file maintained with the investment control log

Investment Gain/Loss Calculation Worksheet

Date _____   Investment number _____

Investment Type
        Description   _____

Original Purchase Price   _____

Premium (subtract) or
    Discount (add)
    Amortization   _____

Amortized Cost at   / /   _____

Less Valuation Allowance   _____

Net Carrying Value   _____

Gross Sales Proceeds   _____

Less Selling Expenses   _____

Net Proceeds   _____

Gain or (Loss)   _____

Comments

_____

_____

_____

	Signature	Title	Date
Preparer	_____	_____	_____
Authorization	_____	_____	_____

Safekeeping Receipt Form

Date _____

From _____

We received/released (description of security) _____

_____

_____

_____

Security was received/delivered from/to _____

_____

_____

Authorized Signature _____

Title _____

Interest Income Worksheet

Investment Number	Description	Date Acquired Month/Year	Interest Rate	Face Amount	Interest Accrual at	Earnings	Receipts	Interest Accrual at

Dividend Earnings Worksheet

Investment Number	Description	Record Date	Dividend Per Share	Number of Shares	Dividends Receivable at	Dividends Earned	Received	Dividends Received at

Appropriations Request Form

Appropriation # _____

Description of
Expenditure

Department to Be
Charged _____

Cash Requirements _____

Budgeted Amount _____

Present Value of
Discounted
Cash Flows

Over (Under)
Budget _____

Date Cash
Is Needed _____

# of Other
Attachments

_____
(Authorizing Signature)

_____
(Title)

_____
(Date)

Detailed Fixed Asset Ledger

Prepared by	...../...../.....
Approved by	...../...../.....

Company ....
Year end: ..../...../.........

	DATE	CLASSIFICATION	1 BALANCE AT BEGINNING OF PERIOD	2 ADDITIONS	3 DISPOSALS	4 OTHER	5 BALANCE AT END OF PERIOD
1							
2							
3							
4							
5							
6							
7							
8							
9							
10							
11							
12							
13							
14							
15							
16							
17							
18							
19							
20							
21							
22							
23							
24							
25							
26							
27							
28							
29							
30							
31							
32							
33							
34							
35							
36							

		CLASSIFICATION	── 1 ── BALANCE AT BEGINNING OF PERIOD	── 2 ── ADDITIONS	── 3 ── DISPOSALS	── 4 ── OTHER	── 5 ── BALANCE AT END OF PERIOD
1							
2							
3							
4							
5							
6							
7							
8							
9							
10							
11							
12							
13							
14							
15							
16							
17							
18							
19							
20							
21							
22							
23							
24							
25							
26							
27							
28							
29							
30							
31							
32							
33							
34							
35							
36							

Disposal Form

Company _____

Tag # of Property Disposed	_____		Reason for Disposal	_____	
Description	_____			_____	
Year of Acquisition	_____			_____	

Original Cost   _____   (a)   Tax Basis   _____   (d)   ITC Recapture

Accumulated Depreciation   _____   (b)   Tax Accumulated Depreciation   _____   (e)   _____

Net Book Value   _____   (a – b)   Tax Net Book Value   _____   (d – e)

Proceeds/Scrap Value*   _____   (c)   Proceeds/Scrap Value*   _____   (f)

Book (Gain) Loss   _____   (a – b – c)   Tax (Gain) Loss   _____   (d – e – f)

*Net of disposal costs.

_____
(Authorizing Signature)

_____
(Title)

_____
(Date)

Requisition Form

		PURCHASE ORDER NUMBER

REQUISITION

CONTROL NUMBER

TO:

VENDOR	VENDOR NO.
NAME	
ADDRESS	
	ZIP

DATE ORDERED	DATE REQUIRED	SHIP TO	SHIP VIA	ON ARRIVAL NOTIFY

INVENTORY	ITEM	QTY.	U/M	DESCRIPTION	UNIT PRICE	TOTAL

SUBMITTED BY	DATE	APPROVED BY	DATE	RECEIVED BY	DATE

ORIGINAL

Approval Limit Schedule

Company Name _____

SPENDING AUTHORIZATION LIMITS

Effective _____
Date

(in Thousands)

Dollar Limits	.5	1	2	3	5	10	25
President	X	X	X	X	X	X	X
Vice-Presidents	X	X	X	X	X	X	
Directors	X	X	X	X	X	X	
General Managers (Purchasing Supervisor)	X	X					
Asst. General Managers	X						
Managers	X						
Supervisors	X						

Purchase Order

PURCHASE ORDER

ABOVE ORDER NO. MUST
APPEAR ON ALL PAPERS
AND PACKAGES RELATIVE
TO THIS ORDER, INCLUD-
ING CORRESPONDENCE

INVOICE IN TRIPLICATE TO

☐ SEE ABOVE   ☐ SAME AS SHIP TO BELOW

VENDOR   **SHIP TO**

REQUISITIONER   DEPARTMENT

ORDER DATE	ENGAGEMENT NUMBER	SHIP VIA	PAYMENT TERMS	DELIVERY DATE

ITEM NO.	QUANTITY	DESCRIPTION	UNIT PRICE	TOTAL

BY

AUTHORIZED SIGNATURE

Receiving Report—description and quantity manually written

RECEIVING RECORD

RECEIVED
FROM:

DATE _____

PO NO. _____

PS NO. _____

Vendor # _____

#	Qty.	Part No.	Description	Account	Price

Comments: _____

_____

POSTED BY: _____   DELIVER TO: _____

INSPECTED BY: _____   DATE: _____

Receiving Report

PURCHASE ORDER

ABOVE ORDER NO. MUST
APPEAR ON ALL PAPERS
AND PACKAGES RELATIVE
TO THIS ORDER, INCLUD-
ING CORRESPONDENCE

INVOICE IN TRIPLICATE TO

☐ SEE ABOVE   ☐ SAME AS SHIP TO BELOW

VENDOR   SHIP TO

REQUISITIONER   DEPARTMENT

ORDER DATE	ENGAGEMENT NUMBER	SHIP VIA	PAYMENT TERMS	DELIVERY DATE
ITEM NO.	QUANTITY	DESCRIPTION	UNIT PRICE	TOTAL

BY

AUTHORIZED SIGNATURE

DATE	NO.	Quan. Rec'd.	Bal. Due	QUALITY	Inspected By	DATE	NO.	Quan. Rec'd.	Bal. Due	QUALITY	Inspected By

Receiving Control Log

RECEIVING LOG

DATE _____

Rec. No.	P.O. #	Vendor	Description	Quantity

Voucher Sheet

Voucher Number _____

Vendor Number _____

Invoice Date _____ $_____

Due Date _____

Gross Amount   Discount

_____

Account No.   Amount

_____

Extensions Checked _____

Columns Footed _____

Purchasing Approval _____

Receiving Report _____

Freight _____

_____

Prepared by   Approved by

Materials Rejection Report

MATERIALS REJECTION REPORT

Responsibility: Supervisor

Name of Vendor _____

Description _____

Cat/Part # _____   Purchase Order # _____

Department _____   Date Received _____

Quantity Received _____   Quantity Rejected _____

Reason for Rejection _____

_____

_____

_____
Signature

Debit Memorandum

Debit Memo

No.

DATE:

PLEASE FORWARD NEW INVOICE
AT TIME OF RESHIPMENT

V
E
N
D
O
R

ATT. ACCOUNTS RECEIVABLE

THE FOLLOWING MATERIAL DOES NOT CONFORM TO THE DRAWING AND/OR SPECIFICATIONS ON OUR P.O. NO.

P.O. NUMBER	DATE RECEIVED	MRA NO.	AUTHORIZED BY	CREDIT ONLY ☐ DO NOT REPLACE	REPLACEMENT REQUIRED BY

ITEM	DESCRIPTION OF MATERIAL	PART NO.	QUANTITY REJECTED	PRICE	EXTENSION

REASON FOR REJECTION

Personnel Action Form

DATED _____

NAME _____

ADDRESS _____

CITY _____

DEPARTMENT _____

SEX ☐ M ☐ F   DATE OF HIRE _____   EMPLOYEE NO. _____

SOC. SEC. NO. _____

HOME PHONE NO. (____) _____

JOB TITLE _____

☐ WAGE ☐ SALARY   **PRESENT RATE** _____ /HR _____ /WEEK

TYPE OF CHANGE

☐ NEW HIRE   ☐ RESIGNATION   ☐ RATE CHANGE
☐ REHIRE   ☐ DISCHARGE   ☐ JOB CHANGE
☐ RETURN FROM LEAVE   ☐ LEAVE OF ABSENCE   ☐ DEPT. CHANGE
☐ OTHER

CHANGED TO

☐ WAGE ☐ SALARY   RATE _____ /HR. _____ /WEEK

JOB TITLE _____
DEPARTMENT _____
OTHER _____

} **EFFECTIVE**

REASON FOR CHANGE _____

REMARKS _____

INITIATED BY _____

APPROVED BY _____

PERSONNEL _____

TOOLS AND STORES CLEARED ☐ **BY** _____   / /

ID BADGE RETURNED ☐ **BY** _____   / /

ELIGIBLE FOR REHIRE _____

Time Card

Company
Time Card

DEPT.   EMP. NO.

_____   _____

FROM _____   TO _____

SIGNED _____

SAT	SUN	MON	TUES	WED	THURS	FRI

Time Sheet

Company
Employee Time Sheet

NAME				SIGNED			
FROM				TO			

JOB #	SAT	MON	TUES	WED	THURS	FRI	TOTAL HOURS
INDIRECT							
OFFICE							
SICKNESS HOLIDAY							
TOTAL HOURS							
SUPPER ALLOWANCE							

NOTES   SEE OVER ☐

1. ENTER HOURS WORKED IN 1/4 HOUR INCREMENTS.
2. THE TOTAL WORK HOURS SHOWN HERE AS WORKED EACH DAY MUST EQUAL THE TOTAL HOURS ACTUALLY WORKED EACH DAY WITH DUE REGARD FOR OVERTIME, LATENESS, TIME OFF, ETC.
3. SIGNED TIME SHEETS MUST BE SUBMITTED NOT LATER THAN 5:15 P.M. FRIDAY AFTERNOON

APPD _____

PART III

APPENDIXES

Appendix A

SAMPLE FINANCIAL STATEMENTS

ABC SERVICE COMPANY
BALANCE SHEET
December 31, 199X

ASSETS:

Current assets:	
Cash and cash equivalents	$ 5,000,000
Accounts receivable, less allowance for doubtful accounts of $240,000	3,000,000
Inventories of supplies, at the lower of cost (first-in, first-out) or market	2,000,000
Prepaid expenses	1,000,000
Total current assets	11,000,000
Fixed assets, at cost, less accumulated depreciation and amortization	9,200,000
Other assets	800,000
	$21,000,000

LIABILITIES:

Current liabilities:	
Accounts payable	$ 1,000,000
Accrued liabilities	2,000,000
Income taxes payable	600,000
Current portion of long-term debt	300,000
Total current liabilities	3,900,000
Long-term debt, less current portion	6,400,000
Other noncurrent liabilities	700,000
	11,000,000

Commitments

STOCKHOLDERS' EQUITY:

Common stock, no par value; authorized, issued, and outstanding 1,000 shares	10,000
Paid-in capital	490,000
Retained earnings	9,500,000
Total stockholders' equity	10,000,000
	$21,000,000

ABC SERVICE COMPANY
STATEMENT of INCOME and RETAINED EARNINGS
for the year ended December 31, 199X

Revenues:	
Service fees	$27,000,000
Conference fees	500,000
Other, net	300,000
	27,800,000
Operating, administrative, and general expenses	24,000,000
Income before provision for income taxes	3,800,000
Provision for income taxes	700,000
Net income	3,100,000
Retained earnings, beginning of year	8,400,000
Distributions to stockholders	(2,000,000)
Retained earnings, end of year	$ 9,500,000

ABC SERVICE COMPANY
STATEMENT of CASH FLOWS
for the year ended December 31, 199X

Cash flows from operating activities:	
Net income	$3,100,000
Adjustments to reconcile net income to net cash provided by operating activities:	
Depreciation and amortization	575,000
Deferred compensation	115,000
	3,790,000
Increase in accounts receivable	(300,000)
Decrease in inventory	600,000
Increase in prepaid expenses	(300,000)
Decrease in income taxes payable	(100,000)
Net cash provided by operating activities	3,690,000
Cash flows from investing activities:	
Acquisition of fixed assets, net	(990,000)
Decrease in other assets	800,000
Net cash used in investing activities	(190,000)
Cash flows from financing activities:	
Payments on debt	(300,000)
Payments of distributions	(2,000,000)
Net cash used in financing activities	(2,300,000)
Net increase in cash and cash equivalents	1,200,000
Cash and cash equivalents at beginning of year	3,800,000
Cash and cash equivalents at end of year	$5,000,000
Supplemental disclosures of cash flow information:	
Cash paid during the year for:	
Interest	$ 400,000
Income taxes	1,000,000

ABC SERVICE COMPANY
SCHEDULE of OPERATING, ADMINISTRATIVE, and GENERAL EXPENSES
for the year ended December 31, 199X

Officers' salaries	$ 985,000
Other salaries, wages, and sales commissions	8,600,000
Incentive compensation	700,000
Savings and pension benefits	550,000
Supplies	470,000
National advertising	630,000
Local advertising	1,265,000
Conference expenses	650,000
Convention	440,000
Promotion	235,000
Travel	915,000
Payroll taxes	730,000
Other taxes, primarily real estate	370,000
Rent	1,220,000
Utilities	215,000
Office and warehouse maintenance	365,000
Depreciation and amortization	570,000
Telephone and telegraph	400,000
Office supplies and expenses	875,000
Postage expense	520,000
Insurance	880,000
Provision for doubtful accounts	65,000
Professional services	1,500,000
Interest	560,000
Contributions	60,000
Directors' fees	38,000
Research and development	72,000
Other	120,000
	$24,000,000

XYZ RETAIL COMPANY and SUBSIDIARY
CONSOLIDATED BALANCE SHEET
December 31, 199X

ASSETS:

Current assets:

Cash	$ 800,000
Sundry receivables	50,000
Merchandise inventory	8,000,000
Due from affiliate	200,000
Prepaid expenses	550,000
Total current assets	9,600,000
Fixed assets, net	3,000,000
Investment in affiliate	1,200,000
Security deposits and other assets	175,000
Cash surrender value of officers' life insurance policies, net of loans	25,000
Total assets	$14,000,000

LIABILITIES:

Current liabilities:

Accounts payable	$ 2,000,000
Current maturities of long-term debt	2,800,000
Current portion of capital lease obligations	130,000
Accrued expenses	400,000
Income taxes payable	570,000
Total current liabilities	5,900,000
Long-term debt	950,000
Long-term portion of capital lease obligations	50,000
Accrued rent	600,000
Total liabilities	7,500,000

STOCKHOLDERS' EQUITY:

Common stock, $1 par value; authorized 75,000 shares; issued and outstanding 25,000 shares	25,000
Additional paid-in capital	175,000
Retained earnings	7,600,000
	7,800,000
Less, Treasury stock, at cost, 30,000 shares	1,300,000
Total stockholders' equity	6,500,000
Total liabilities and stockholders' equity	$14,000,000

XYZ RETAIL COMPANY and SUBSIDIARY
CONSOLIDATED STATEMENT of INCOME and RETAINED EARNINGS
for the year ended December 31, 199X

Net sales	$45,000,000
Cost of goods sold	27,000,000
Gross profit	18,000,000
Store expenses	15,000,000
Income from store operations	3,000,000
General and administrative expenses	2,500,000
Operating income	500,000
Other income (expense):	
Interest income	75,000
Interest expense	(515,000)
Rental income	65,000
Miscellaneous income	20,000
	(355,000)
Income before provision for income taxes	145,000
Provision for income taxes	15,000
Net income	130,000
Retained earnings, beginning of year	7,470,000
Retained earnings, end of year	$ 7,600,000

XYZ RETAIL COMPANY and SUBSIDIARY
CONSOLIDATED STATEMENT of CASH FLOWS
for the year ended December 31, 199X

Cash flows from operating activities:	
Net income	$ 130,000
Adjustments to reconcile net income to net cash provided by operating activities:	
Depreciation and amortization	900,000
Accrued rent	170,000
Changes in assets and liabilities:	
Increase in sundry receivables	(27,000)
Increase in prepaid expenses	(120,000)
Decrease in security deposits and other assets	35,000
Increase in cash surrender value of officers' life insurance	(5,000)
Increase in accounts payable	1,810,000
Decrease in accrued expenses	(138,000)
Increase in income taxes payable	45,000
Net cash provided by operating activities	2,800,000
Cash flows from investing activities:	
Purchase of fixed assets, net	(1,100,000)
Net cash used for investing activities	(1,100,000)
Cash flows from financing activities:	
Repayments of borrowings:	
Loans	(880,000)
Capital lease obligations	(140,000)
Amounts due from affiliate	(480,000)
Note payable to stockholder	(100,000)
Net cash used for financing activities	(1,600,000)
Net increase in cash	100,000
Cash at beginning of year	700,000
Cash at end of year	$ 800,000

XYZ RETAIL COMPANY and SUBSIDIARY
SCHEDULE OF COST OF GOODS SOLD
for the year ended December 31, 199X

Merchandise inventory, beginning of year	$ 8,000,000
Merchandise inventory purchases and inward freight	28,000,000
Less: Purchase discounts	(1,000,000)
Net cost of purchases	27,000,000
Total cost of merchandise inventory available for sale	35,000,000
Less: Merchandise inventory, end of year	8,000,000
Cost of goods sold	$27,000,000

XYZ RETAIL COMPANY and SUBSIDIARY
SCHEDULE OF STORE EXPENSES
for the year ended December 31, 199X

Cost of occupancy	$ 4,800,000
Payroll	4,700,000
Advertising	2,000,000
Depreciation and amortization	700,000
Services, maintenance, etc.	700,000
Miscellaneous store expenses	600,000
Charge card expenses	500,000
Payroll taxes	300,000
Insurance	300,000
Wrapping and shipping supplies	100,000
Employees' benefit expense	150,000
Telephone and telegraph	120,000
Miscellaneous taxes	30,000
	$15,000,000

XYZ RETAIL COMPANY and SUBSIDIARY
SCHEDULE OF GENERAL AND ADMINISTRATIVE EXPENSES
for the year ended December 31, 199X

General and administrative salaries	$ 750,000
Officers' salaries	500,000
Office supplies and expenses	300,000
Professional services	200,000
Travel and auto expenses	90,000
Depreciation and amortization	180,000
Payroll taxes	130,000
Office rent	100,000
Life insurance premiums	100,000
Employees' welfare expense	80,000
Telephone and telegraph	50,000
Meals and entertainment	15,000
Contributions	5,000
	$2,500,000

ACE MANUFACTURING CORPORATION
BALANCE SHEET
December 31, 199X

ASSETS:

Cash	$ 500,000
Accounts receivable, net	7,400,000
Inventories	12,000,000
Prepaid expenses and other assets	200,000
Deferred taxes	150,000
Total current assets	20,250,000
Property, plant, and equipment, net	4,750,000
Deferred taxes	40,000
Other assets	60,000
Total assets	$25,100,000

LIABILITIES and STOCKHOLDERS' EQUITY:

Notes payable	$ 300,000
Current installments of long-term debt and capital lease obligations	400,000
Accounts payable and accrued expenses	5,700,000
Accrued salaries and withholdings	500,000
Dividend payable	300,000
Due to affiliate	1,200,000
Total current liabilities	8,400,000
Long-term debt and capital lease obligations, net of current installments	1,600,000
Total liabilities	10,000,000

Commitments

Stockholders' equity:

Common stock, $10 par value; 10,000 shares authorized, issued and outstanding	100,000
Paid-in capital	9,600,000
Retained earnings	5,400,000
Total stockholder's equity	15,100,000
Total liabilities and stockholders' equity	$25,100,000

ACE MANUFACTURING CORPORATION
STATEMENT OF INCOME and RETAINED EARNINGS
for the year ended December 31, 199X

Net sales	$59,000,000
Cost of sales:	
Finished goods inventories, beginning of year	10,800,000
Cost of goods manufactured	37,200,000
Other manufacturing costs	12,000,000
	60,000,000
Finished goods inventories, end of year	12,000,000
Cost of sales	48,000,000
Gross profit	11,000,000
Selling, general, and administrative expenses	8,000,000
Income from operations	3,000,000
Other income (expense):	
Interest expense	(900,000)
Interest income	20,000
	(880,000)
Income before provision for income taxes	2,120,000
Provision for income taxes	1,000,000
Net income	1,120,000
Retained earnings, beginning of year	4,580,000
Dividends	(300,000)
Retained earnings, end of year	$ 5,400,000

ACE MANUFACTURING CORPORATION
STATEMENT of CASH FLOWS
for the year ended December 31, 199X

Cash flows from operating activities:	
Net income	$1,120,000
Adjustments to reconcile net income to net cash provided by operating activities:	
Depreciation and amortization	1,300,000
Changes in assets and liabilities:	
Decrease in accounts receivable	2,000,000
Increase in inventory	(1,500,000)
Increase in income taxes receivable	(100,000)
Increase in prepaid expenses	(300,000)
Increase in other assets	(20,000)
Decrease in accounts payable and accrued expenses	(1,400,000)
Decrease in deferred taxes	(300,000)
Decrease in accrued salaries and related withholding	(20,000)
Total adjustments	(340,000)
Net cash provided by operating activities	780,000
Cash flows used by investing activities:	
Acquisition of property, plant, and equipment	(500,000)
Net cash used by investing activities	(500,000)
Cash flows used by financing activities:	
Repayment of long-term debt	(70,000)
Proceeds of note payable under line of credit	300,000
Principal payments under lease obligations	(310,000)
Net cash used by financing activities	(80,000)
Net decrease in cash and cash equivalents	200,000
Cash at beginning of year	300,000
Cash at end of year	$ 500,000

ACE MANUFACTURING CORPORATION
SCHEDULE of COST of GOODS MANUFACTURED
for the year ended December 31, 199X

Raw materials:	
Raw materials inventory, beginning of year	$10,000,000
Purchases of raw materials	19,200,000
Raw materials inventory, end of year	(12,000,000)
Raw materials used in manufacturing	17,200,000
Direct labor:	
Salaries and wages	6,600,000
Payroll taxes	2,000,000
Insurance and benefits	1,400,000
Subtotal direct labor	10,000,000
Labor applied to inventory	(150,000)
Total direct labor	9,850,000
Manufacturing overhead:	
Indirect labor	2,000,000
Supplies	900,000
Other operating costs	2,000,000
Outside services	3,000,000
Allocated occupancy expenses	1,300,000
Depreciation and amortization	1,200,000
Subtotal manufacturing overhead	10,400,000
Manufacturing overhead applied	(250,000)
Total manufacturing overhead	10,150,000
Cost of goods manufactured	$37,200,000

KEY BUSINESS RATIOS AND OTHER ANALYTICAL MEASUREMENTS

SUMMARY OF KEY BUSINESS RATIOS AND OTHER ANALYTICAL MEASUREMENTS

Many groups outside the business enterprise—creditors, investors, financial analysts, and regulatory agencies—are interested in the financial affairs of a company. Outsiders do not always have access to detailed information about a company and must therefore rely on published information available from other sources. Typically, this information regarding a company's performance is measured and compared through financial ratios.

Key business ratios are as follows:

Quick (acid-test) ratio

Computation: $$\frac{\text{Current assets less inventory}}{\text{Current liabilities}}$$

Significance: Reveals the protection afforded short-term creditors by the most liquid current assets. The larger the ratio, the greater the liquidity.

Inventory turnover

Computation: $$\frac{\text{Cost of goods sold}}{\text{Average inventory}}$$

Significance: Measures the number of times inventory turns over during the year. Generally, this expresses management's ability to control the investment in inventory; however, seasonal fluctuations should be taken into account.

Days in inventory

Computation: $$\frac{365}{\text{Inventory Turnover}}$$

Significance: Indicates the average number of days that units are in inventory.

Debt to equity

Computation: $$\frac{\text{Total liabilities}}{\text{Tangible net worth}}$$

Significance: Indicates the relationship between borrowed capital and invested capital. In general, total liabilities should not exceed net worth since in such case creditors have more at stake than owners.

Current ratio

Computation:
$$\frac{\text{Current assets}}{\text{Current liabilities}}$$

Significance: Measures the degree of the company's ability to service its current obligations. Normally, a ratio of 2 to 1 is considered good.

Receivables turnover

Computation:
$$\frac{\text{Net sales}}{\text{Average receivables}}$$

Significance: Measures the number of times receivables turn over during the year. The higher the turnover, the shorter the time between the sale and the collection.

Days in receivables

Computation:
$$\frac{365}{\text{Receivables turnover}}$$

Significance: Indicates the average number of days that receivables are outstanding. Generally, this expresses the effectiveness of collections; however, industry terms should be taken into consideration.

Return on net worth

Computation:
$$\frac{\text{Net income}}{\text{Average net worth}}$$

Significance: Indicates the earnings power of the capital invested. Generally, a relationship of at least 10 percent is regarded as a desirable objective for providing dividends plus funds for future growth.

Return on assets

Computation:
$$\frac{\text{Net income}}{\text{Average total assets}}$$

Significance: Measures the productivity of assets. Companies efficiently using their assets will have a relatively high return while that of less well run businesses will be relatively low.

Price–earnings ratio on common stock

Computation: $$\frac{\text{Market price per share}}{\text{Earnings per share}}$$

Significance: Indicates whether the price of the stock is in line with earnings.

Book value per share

Computation: $$\frac{\text{Stockholders' equity}}{\text{Shares of stock outstanding}}$$

Significance: Measures the amount of net assets that are applicable to each share of stock.

Appendix C

COMPUTER SYSTEMS SELECTION AND IMPLEMENTATION*

* Pages 317-350 reprinted by permission
of John Wiley & Sons, Inc.

COMPUTER SYSTEMS SELECTION AND IMPLEMENTATION

Once your accounting system has developed to the point where the procedural cycles are more or less continuous operations or your present data processing equipment is nearing the end of its useful life, you should begin to think about the possibility of investing in, replacing, or upgrading your computer system. As your business continues to grow, it is not unlikely that your present system will begin to show strain. Even before that happens, you may find that you cannot get timely information to help manage important operational matters such as inventory control or product-line profitability, or the data needed to improve customer service.

Technological advances, competition, the need for quick access to accurate business information, and reductions in the cost of hardware and software have stimulated many emerging businesses to invest in computerized systems. As a result, businesspeople who may not have the technical expertise to undertake feasibility studies or computer hardware evaluations are being asked to make decisions regarding the purchase and selection of computers. Mastering the basic terminology is simply not enough to enable them to decide wisely. Take, for example, these common problems:

- Choosing an unnecessarily expensive and complex computer system
- Using a computer system for data that would be better processed by improved manual or semimechanized methods
- Choosing a computer that cannot be easily expanded to accommodate additional work
- Delegating systems development to staff who lack the proper technical skills or business understanding
- Choosing a computer with poor vendor support or inappropriate processing techniques

To help the emerging business manager avoid these pitfalls, this discussion focuses on six important areas—the value of a computer to your business, the computer environment, how to select the right computer, the costs of computer systems, the installation process, and procedures and controls for computer systems. By following the general guidelines given here, a businessperson will be better equipped to assess computer needs, make informed decisions about appropriate equipment, and help ensure continued functioning of the computer with adequate controls.

The Value of a Computer to Your Business

People first think of installing business computers because they feel instinctively that cost savings and efficiency improvements might be achieved or they see that existing manual systems are strained or that current computer equipment is nearing the end of its useful life. Particular management problems such as inadequate information for accounts receivable or inventory control, or the need for improved customer service may indicate that a new approach to information processing is needed.

Features Most Adaptable to Computerization

The features of a company's business that are usually computerized rely on the special characteristics of the computer, such as:

- the ability to carry out, accurately and quickly, simple tasks such as price calculations or wage calculations,
- the capacity to store a large amount of data and use it easily for analysis and processing,
- the ability to transfer common data among different systems (e.g., sales order information may be fed directly through a production planning and stock system to a sales accounting system and general ledger), and
- the potential for relieving staff of routine tasks

Although these accounting and production control operations are the ones that first come to mind, other specialized repetitive jobs equally suited to a small computer include general accounting, mailing lists, personnel records, vehicle scheduling, and even word processing.

Benefits

Computer systems can yield considerable benefits:

- In order processing, quicker deliveries and more accurate order statistics
- In accounts receivable, faster routine billing and collections
- In inventory, reduced inventory investment and an improved inventory availability
- In purchasing, better cash management and an improved purchasing history
- In payroll, faster calculations and improved analysis of costs
- In general ledger accounting, more timely management reports
- In production planning, better use of labor production facilities

Evaluating Your Computer Needs

Initially, you will have two questions to answer in connection with automation: First, Do I need it? and second, If so, how much and what kind? These questions are not easy to answer; they require study and, unless you have a good knowledge of computerized accounting, a certain amount of expert assistance. If you act hastily, you risk committing a potentially costly blunder.

Preliminary Survey. Before beginning a detailed investigation of your computer needs, you need to establish the objectives you want to achieve. The reasons for considering computerization and the possible benefits should be set down in writing, taking into account overall business objectives, identifying high priority areas, and establishing cost parameters.

One of the major advantages of computers with integrated software is combining separate clerical tasks and reducing duplication of information. For instance, once sales invoices are recorded in an invoicing application, the data can be reused for sales accounting and sales analysis without reinputting the information. So during the preliminary survey you should consider all applications related to priority areas; otherwise, systems can quickly outgrow the equipment as the opportunities for linking with other areas are understood. The preliminary review will identify:

- the reasons for considering computerization,
- the overall objectives and the expected benefits,
- the application areas to be examined, and
- the cost justification for the system.

Feasibility Study. If the preliminary survey is positive, your next step will be to carry out a more detailed feasibility study; the main objectives here are to determine if computerization will work, will be useful, and is economically worth doing. Your feasibility study should include:

- an analysis of present systems, highlighting strengths and weaknesses,
- a detailed written outline of how the proposed systems will work so that company managers and personnel can understand and agree to the implications of the system,
- an analysis of current and projected data volumes,
- a proposed implementation timetable, and
- estimates of the costs and benefits of the new systems.

No decision to replace an existing procedure with a computer system should be made without considering whether the same benefits would be more easily or inexpensively obtained in other ways. For example, it may be that redesigning forms and clerical procedures or improving filing systems and the layout of offices and workflows would be better than computerization.

You also run the risk that without a good understanding of the different types of computer and processing facilities, the system features developed and the related costs may be inappropriate for your organization. The natural tendency is to avoid the problem by calling in one or more computer suppliers. Although this seems a good way of obtaining free advice, computer salespeople often recommend an approach that demonstrates the best features of their own equipment but that is not necessarily the most suitable or cost-effective for your company. Ideally, therefore, you should not seek the advice of computer salespeople until you have a good understanding of your requirements. If expert advice is required, you should consider going to independent consultants who have no affiliation to software or hardware manufacturers or suppliers.

How to Select the Right Computer

Your initial investigations will have determined the system and general type of computer facility you require. You will also have made a choice between a service bureau and an in-house computer. Your next step is to invite your selected suppliers to present their proposals.

To avoid future misunderstandings and to provide a consistent basis for comparing proposals, you must give the suppliers a written statement of requirements. This should contain:

- a brief description of the company, the existing processing systems, and the environment in which the system must operate;
- a description of the main purpose and features of each system required;
- an indication of the volume and content of each of the input documents and output reports and, where necessary, a description of the intermediate processing steps to clarify the logic of any complex requirements;
- current and projected data volumes;
- an itemized statement of information on costs, time frames, maintenance, experience, and staffing that must be included in the suppliers' proposal.

The initial selection of suppliers invited to propose can present problems. Many specialist firms have developed links with computer manufacturers so that they act as prime contractors, offering both equipment and programs. These firms are usually referred to as "systems houses."

The result of this proliferation of suppliers has been to dramatically increase the choices facing a potential purchaser. There is a risk that you will waste time obtaining quotations from suppliers with inappropriate equipment or that you will omit suppliers with extremely suitable equipment and services from your proposal list; so again, consider getting expert independent advice or consult with other business associates.

The Choice of Software

Closely linked to the selection of an equipment supplier is the choice of a method for developing the applications software. There are essentially three choices:

- Your organization can employ systems analysts and programmers and establish an in-house systems development capability.
- The computer supplier or a systems house can be contracted to undertake the systems and programming or supply off-the-shelf applications software.
- The systems and programming implementation can be directed by management consultants retained separately from the equipment contract.

Few small organizations will want to recruit their own systems analyst and programmers, especially if the systems have to be developed quickly. For this reason, the trend is toward using outside specialists. There are benefits in dealing with only one contractor, but a major disadvantage is that the supplier of the best hardware is frequently not the organization with the skills and experience to understand your systems requirements or to design and implement a solution to your problem. In fact, many computer manufacturers do not offer systems development support and instead refer customers to systems houses.

Evaluating Proposals

You should give suppliers a reasonable time in which to submit their proposals. You then need to assess the proposals using a set of criteria that relate to:

- the adequacy of the proposed equipment to process the current and planned workload within defined time limits
- the adequacy of the proposed terminal response times
- the ability to expand components of the equipment to handle increased workloads
- the versatility, reliability, and ease of use of those computer programs (systems software) supplied with the equipment to control its operation
- the bidders' understanding of the application system requirements and their approach to system design
- the flexibility, suitability, and user history of any proposed engineering packages
- the reliability of the equipment and the quality of engineering maintenance

- the value of the total services offered, recognizing that the lowest price is not necessarily the best

Selecting a Service Bureau

To select a service bureau, you should follow a path similar to that described above, asking several bureaus to quote against a definition of requirements. The criteria to use for selection are also similar, but you should consider in addition the convenience and quality of the day-to-day operational service provided. Provision of contingency facilities and the degree of experience in your industry are also important.

Costs of a Computer System

Hardware

A computer capable of providing on-line processing through two terminals can be purchased for under $20,000. This basic price will normally be the figure initially quoted by the salesman to secure customer interest. However, essential additional expenses—for purchasing or developing systems and their associated programs—will increase this cost.

In common with other electronic products, such as pocket calculators and digital watches, the cost of computer equipment continues to decrease steadily. Unfortunately, the costs of developing the systems and programs have not followed this trend, and in common with other skill-based resources, these costs will probably continue to increase. The cost of developing a customized series of accounting systems on a small business computer will rarely be less than $25,000 and is frequently greater than the price of the equipment itself. The key factor is the complexity of the system requirements and the resulting effort needed to embody the logic of the system into a set of computer programs. There is no fixed relationship between the computer and software costs.

Although the costs of developing systems and programs appear high, the ultimate success of any system is more dependent on the quality of the work than on the equipment itself. For this reason, you should not try to make large savings in this area, since correcting any errors and shortcomings in the original system can be expensive.

Standard Packages

In order to help overcome the high cost of systems development work, certain equipment suppliers and specialist firms have developed standard packages for the more common processing applications. The packages may be purchased or leased for considerably less than it would cost to develop a customized system. Usually, no single package completely suits a particular organization's requirements, and the company may want to revise procedures to fit the package or modify it for special requirements—but this can be as costly as developing a unique system if the changes are more than merely cosmetic.

Hidden Costs

Apart from the costs for systems development and programming, there are other expenses to consider:

- Specialist staff—Even if development is subcontracted to a software house, you should assign an operator/manager to coordinate with the software house and consultants and to provide a degree of professional in-house expertise.
- Engineering maintenance—This has traditionally run about 10 percent annually of the capital hardware costs for normal operation and can rise sharply if maintenance is done outside regular office hours.
- Software maintenance—Systems and program maintenance for minor changes and extensions will recur and can be expensive.
- Installation and room preparation—This is normally a minor cost, but in certain situations you may need to purchase an air conditioner and storage cabinets and install a special electrical circuit to avoid voltage fluctuation.

Installation Process

When you have concluded the lengthy discussions leading to the decision to install a computer system and to select a particular supplier, there is a natural tendency to relax. Nothing could be more dangerous. It is in the next few months that the success or failure of the project will be determined.

Having chosen your system and your contractors, you are ready to enter the installation phase of computerization. This is a difficult period not only in a technical but also in a human sense. Computer equipment interfaces with people, and in certain circumstances, people have trouble getting used to it. It is important, therefore, to proceed cautiously; obstacles that arise in this period tend to be difficult to remove later.

Unless the development phase proceeds with senior management involvement and encouragement, it is all too easy for the installed system to be inadequate, implementation delayed, and the user staff ill-prepared. Any barriers and prejudices created in these circumstances may be extremely difficult to remove. In most organizations, the development phase should be controlled by naming an overall manager and, when appropriate, obtaining professional assistance on a scheduled basis. The manager is responsible for approving a detailed development and implementation plan for the installation phase.

A typical installation plan consists of the following tasks:

- Specification of user requirements in each of the areas to be computerized
- Agreement to and acceptance of the specification by the users
    Design of supporting clerical procedures
    Production of a system and program specifications
    Preparation of computer programs
- Preparation of user instructions
- Site preparation and installation of facilities such as:
    Communications systems
    Air conditioning
    Electrical connections and cabling
    Fire prevention and safety equipment
    Security systems
    Computer room furniture
- Installation of computer equipment
- Equipment acceptance testing
- Training of user staff
- Preparation of computer operating instructions
- Systems testing and analysis of systems test results
- Creation of computer master files
- Pilot and parallel running of each system and checking of results by users
- Systems acceptance by users
- Postimplementation review

Remember, with careful planning you can avoid costly mistakes.

One of the major challenges to face when you automate is setting up controls to curb errors in and to prevent fraudulent manipulation of your automated procedures.

A business computer system requires more specific controls than does a large one. As previously discussed, like their counterparts in middle-sized and large organizations, smaller systems often incorporate integrated applications with on-line, that is, directly linked to the computer, input, processing, and updating of data files. Yet typically, the atmosphere of a small operation is informal and frequently involves multifunctions performed by one person. There may be difficulty keeping unauthorized persons away from the computer. In addition, small operations seldom have much in-house technical capability, so they cannot rely to the same degree as better-staffed, larger operations on ad hoc investigations to review their automated activities.

How Consultants Can Help

The introduction of a computer system into an organization should be smooth; the aim is to ensure that the entire procedure is completed without disruption of day-to-day activities or creation of major problems. To achieve this objective, management must make these decisions:

- Agree that a computer system is necessary
- Select the applications that can benefit from being computer based
- Select the most suitable processing philosophy (e.g., batch processing or on-line, in-house computer or service bureau)
- Select the computer supplier best able to provide and maintain equipment matched to the application requirements
- Arrange for the system design and programming to be carried out by those with technical understanding of the chosen computer, an appreciation of the business and the ability to deliver systems on time and within budget
- Allocate sufficient top management time to all stages of the project—with emphasis on participation during system design—to ensure preparedness and commitment when the system goes live

Given the importance of these decisions, there are advantages to seeking expert advice if the company has no previous experience in this area. During the feasibility study, a consultant can help you answer these questions:

- Is a computer really needed?
- If so, what areas in the organization will benefit the most?
- What is the processing philosophy?
- What are the priorities and time frame for installation?
- How much will it cost?
- What benefits can be expected?

Then, once agreement has been reached on getting a computer, a consultant can help select the right vendor by:

- preparing a statement of requirements and a formal request for proposal,
- reviewing proposals for both software and hardware,
- selecting a vendor,
- advising on contractual questions

During implementation, a consultant's assistance can be at three levels:

1. At the lowest level, the role is purely advisory, alerting management to danger signals that indicate problems at a later date if proper action is not taken.

2. At an intermediate level, support can be extended to include the design of the computer systems and supporting clerical procedures. In this situation, a consultant prepares user specifications for agreement with management, designs report formats, supervises systems testing, arranges for file conversion, and trains the staff.

3. At the highest level, the consultant provides a complete implementation service by selecting and monitoring the programming effort in addition to the tasks described above. Under this arrangement, the consultant takes project responsibility from systems design through staff training.

Drawing on related experience in similar technical and industry fields, consultants can apply a fresh and independent view to problems that individual companies may be facing for the first time. Consultants are also well equipped to approach questions on the introduction of computers from the businessperson's viewpoint in order to ensure that computers are used in ways that will bring the greatest benefits. And consultants can help avoid the pitfalls that so many nontechnical managers face as they judge their computer needs.

Appendix D

THREE-WAY BUDGET: THE ASPECTS OF CASH MANAGEMENT*

* Reprinted by permission of
John Wiley & Sons, Inc.

THREE-WAY BUDGET:
THE ASPECTS OF CASH MANAGEMENT

Introduction

There are many reasons for the successful transformation from a small or medium-sized company into a large one: a changing economy, altered consumer habits, development of a superior product or service, even the luck of being in the right business at the right time. But one factor is common to all such successes—the company is well managed.

At Coopers & Lybrand, we're fortunate in having helped many companies grow and, in the process, having learned a great deal about a company's management needs on the way up. Among those needs are effective planning and control, including cash management, which encourage prudent operation based on realistic financial conditions.

Our Firm's involvement in helping an owner-manager develop his company during the critical growth period has given us a perspective and discipline that derive from practical experience. We have formulated some of this know-how into a program we call the "three-way budget." The term "three-way" reflects the three basic aspects of cash management: operations, cash flow and financial condition—items so interdependent they must be treated simultaneously. Together, they provide the information an owner-manager needs to run a well-managed business, use his resources effectively and provide himself with data for financial presentation to bankers.

We began developing the three-way budget some fifty years ago. In that half-century much has changed, including some aspects of business and budgeting. But the three-way budget's continuing usefulness can be attributed to its commonsense approach and its easy implementation. As it has worked for others, it can work for you.

PART 1: A GUIDE TO CASH CONTROL

Next to human error, lack of effective control over cash resources is the most common cause of business failure. This is particularly true during the difficult years when small businesses with great potential and expectations frequently fold up simply through lack of judicious cash control.

Paradoxically, prosperity itself is often the problem: flourishing sales entail unexpectedly heavy expenditures for raw materials and payrolls—and your company can find itself with an unbridgeable gap between accounts payable and accounts receivable. With foresight, you could have anticipated that the revenues from the extra sales simply wouldn't be received in time to pay all the extra expenses. But this hindsight isn't enough to persuade bankers to extend additional credit quickly—and so your company folds.

The key is a simple but reliable system that anticipates cash needs and plans adequately to satisfy them. The three-way budget is such a system, used successfully by hundreds of small and medium-sized businesses over the years to help them cope with their liquidity problems and to plan and control month-to-month operations.

Benefits

The three-way budget is useful both internally and externally. The confidence of bankers and agencies extending credit is enhanced when a customer produces a month-by-month operating plan as a guide to actual performance. In turn, that plan serves owner-managers as a road map for more effectively managing their cash.

As a businessman, you'll find the system valuable because each month you'll have:

- A statement of earnings showing how your operating plans for the company will lead to success, a forecast that can be matched against actual results and used to provide warning signals so that corrective action can be taken when necessary
- A statement of cash flow indicating how you plan to handle your company's finances during a critical period in its growth
- A balance sheet allowing you to monitor your company's financial strength on a regular basis.

To the banker, the system is important because it gives him a solid basis for evaluating a loan through:

- A month-by-month projection of earnings, enabling him to compare anticipated income with previous years' and current performance when actual results are available
- A monthly cash-flow statement, enabling him to see when cash will be derived from company operations and when from credit grantors; when the cost of major projects will be paid; and when long-term loans, operating costs and bank loans will be repaid
- A monthly balance sheet showing the company's financial position and indicating the value of the asset security pledged as collateral for loans and advances.

The banker is thus more likely to conclude that your presentation is logical and you are a sound businessman in control of yourself and your resources. So extending a reasonable line of credit seems justified. Contributing to the banker's confidence is the knowledge that he will be able to regularly monitor the progress of your plan.

General Approach and Components

In simple terms, the three-way budget is a cash management system expressing, in dollars on a monthly basis, the strategy you intend to follow to achieve your objectives. You begin by writing a carefully considered statement of those objectives: *This is precisely what I want to do.* You continue with detailed assumptions of the elements needed to bring it about: *This is how I can get it done.* These assumptions include matters like the line of credit you expect, gross profits and expense levels and trends, share of the market and major business developments you anticipate for the coming year. (Part 2 illustrates how to prepare these statements in a case study of the Relentless Pursuits Company.)

The other components of the three-way budget—cost of sales analysis, earnings statement, cash-flow statement and balance sheet—are the four major budget reporting areas. Each is prepared on an annual basis, broken down month by month, for all revenue and expense details. Monthly reports let you monitor each component by comparing actual performance with budget, both for the current month and cumulatively. Three-way budgeting, by assessing for you what is actually happening on a regular basis, keeps you aware of what's going on in your business so you can direct its performance and, if necessary, take any corrective action.

Preparing the First Budget

The first three-way budget for a going concern requires an opening balance sheet and the previous year's results in as much detail as possible. By estimating the expected sales level for the coming year and anticipating any change from the level experienced by the business in the preceding year, you can identify both revenues and expenses with specific month of the coming year.

Anticipated sales are a critical factor in preparing the entire budget because they invariably determine both volume of activity and timing of expenditures. By working backward from these sales for each month, you can determine the outlays required to meet that level of sales and then allow the appropriate lead time between sales and cash collections and between commitments and their eventual payment. In this way, you can identify cash receipts and expenditures with specific months.

The principal point of departure for preparing the budget is the previous year's results, but you must carefully scrutinize those results for factors that may lead to different results in the year ahead. For example, in breaking down annual sales by months, you must assess seasonal fluctuations of volume and product mix as well as additional output of new facilities. In projecting expenses, you must allow for possible increases in raw material costs, supplies and other overhead expenses and for any new capital expenditures, like added equipment or plant facilities.

Breaking down expenses by month requires careful attention to factors that will influence timing. For example, the accrual basis of accounting is used for net income and balance sheet items, but the cash basis is needed to determine cash flow for insurance, professional fees, licenses, commissions and property, business and income taxes, and the like.

Seasonal fluctuations also require attention for expenses related to sales promotions, production, utilities, advertising campaigns, maintenance and vacation costs. Interest and income taxes must be developed monthly because of their direct relationship to bank advances and earnings.

These examples stress that you must give careful attention to the nature of every item of expense—its characteristics and trends—in order to more accurately forecast business results and cash requirements on a month-by-month basis.

For convenience, we have summarized some principal points in the "Instructions for Preparing Projections," beginning on page 340. Although the finished statements are separate, they are closely interrelated and are prepared somewhat in tandem. Everything flows from the basic sales projection and the assumptions about how those sales will be met. So completing the cost of sales and earnings statements provides major elements of information for the cash-flow statement and balance sheet projection.

Monitoring Performance

When the three-way budget is completed, it gives, for a 12-month period, monthly projections of revenues, expenses and account balances in enough detail so you can measure annual performance. The four statements that compare results of actual operations for the current month with the budget for each of the major reporting areas—cost of sales, earnings, cash flow and balance—give you the information you need to assess your company's financial and operational condition. With this knowledge, you can consider taking corrective action any time it's necessary.

Although the three-way budget is frequently used for obtaining credit, its use as an operating plan may be at least as important. Regular feedback of actual performance data, when compared with the budget, offers you a way to monitor and control finances and operations on a day-to-day basis that can frequently make the difference between success and failure. Indeed, even when a business is fortunate enough to operate without outside financing, the three-way budget is a valuable tool for controlling and anticipating situations where recourse to outside financing might be needed.

Much more so than annual budget reporting, monthly budget reporting—in the reasonable amount of detail suggested by this system—assures you that all the major elements influencing actual performance are being considered on a timely basis. You can see how well your company is progressing toward fulfilling your desired goals. Since the budget is no more than a statement of what would happen if observed trends continued and new plans materialized, you must expect variances and deal with them promptly when they arise.

Taking Corrective Action

Variations from plan may be caused by a number of factors. Externally, these may include market conditions, property tax increases, strikes and plant shutdowns, while internally they may involve abnormal maintenance and repairs, idle time, defective production, returned sales and customer and supplier defaults. But whether favorable or unfavorable, controllable or uncontrollable, they demand your swift attention so you can cope with the consequences and plan effectively.

Appropriate interpretation of unfavorable developments is critical, as it becomes the basis for reappraising the situation and deciding on corrective action or protective measures. Correctly interpreting favorable variances, on the other hand, can result in useful revisions to long-term plans, allocation of surplus cash to loan repayments, increased advertising expenditures, temporary investments or a totally new and ambitious marketing program.

Reviewing and Revising the Budget

When the monthly reports show significant changes, you must consider whether to revise the total budget or continue with the basic budget and make the short-term adjustments needed to deal with the variance. While you may find it more useful to make new projections for the balance of the year, preserving the budget with suitable reservations is often preferable. Remember that the three-way budget is only a road map that indicates the direction the company is headed in—it may be unwise to recast the plan every time a roadblock necessitates a detour. As a reflection of the financial objectives of company goals, the budget can remain a useful tool for steering operations back onto the desired course.

The types of deviations that emerge in each month's reports are the principal factors in judging whether to retain the existing budget or totally recast it. Each variance report has space for comments that explain an item's difference from plan so you can decide whether operational changes are substantial enough to require recasting.

Responding to Changes

The three-way budget constitutes both an early-warning system and a frame of reference for evaluating the financial consequences of operational decisions. By revising assumptions in the light of these changing conditions, you and your banker can assess your company's cash position for the rest of the year with relative ease.

No business can be completely ensured against adversity, nor can you expect to be completely free of problems. But by controlling the financial consequences of these problems with a well-designed budgeting system, you're better prepared to respond quickly and effectively to any circumstances.

PART 2: THE STEP-BY-STEP APPROACH

Despite its thoroughness and detail, the three-way budget is simple to prepare. Before you start on one for your own business, follow the steps given here for preparing one for the Relentless Pursuits Company so you can become familiar with the procedure. The company is, of course, fictitious, but the facts, figures and event are taken from actual client situations.

The objectives and assumptions represent the results of many hours spent by the owner-manager in evaluation, market assessment and negotiations with bankers and other lenders. Because the budget is only as good as the assumptions on which it's based, these must be as sound and realistic a reflection of the year's expectations as possible. To make sure this budget will prove effective for managing operations, the owner-manager of Relentless Pursuits gave these matters extremely careful thought.

Objectives

The Relentless Pursuits budget is based on an explicit set of objectives that anticipate a requirement for financing during periods of inadequate cash flow:

1. To continue increased market penetration.
2. To expand physical facilities to meet increased product demand.
3. To improve product quality without increasing unit cost.

Assumptions

To prepare its budget, the company's owner-manager established fundamental assumptions as a basis for assigning revenues, expenses, cash receipts and expenditures to the appropriate periods:

1. $120,000 mortgage loan commitment for a government development agency collateralized by new building facility, payable $5,000 a month beginning in October.

2. Construction costs to be paid in four equal monthly installments.

3. 30% sales increase on an annual basis.

4. 12.5% gross profit margin on sales on an annual basis.

5. 10% increase over previous year in total expenses, including interest expense.

6. First quarter inventory buildup for peak summer sales season.

7. Collection of accounts receivable anticipated to be 40% in month following sale, 50% in subsequent month and 10% in third month.

8. Payments for raw material purchases in January through September anticipated to be 75% in the first month following purchase and 25% in the subsequent months of that period. Payments in October through December anticipated at 100% in the months following purchase.

9. Labor costs and interest expense paid as incurred.

10. Most other expenses paid in the following month after they are incurred.

11. $1,200 a month set aside for estimated income tax payments.

Actual Budget Preparation

By applying all these assumptions to the basic sales expectations, Relentless Pursuits was able to complete the three-way budget as three separate projected monthly financial statements in the three basic categories: cost of sales (Exhibit A), earnings (Exhibit B), and cash flow (Exhibit C).

Using the information provided by these three basic statements, the company produced a balance sheet (Exhibit D) also broken down monthly, creating a presentation that can serve as input to the bank for obtaining and maintaining assured financing.

The information available from the completed budget provides these answers to four critical questions:

1. The year's profit is expected to be $30,680.

2. Cash-flow deficits call for a loan of $133,000 during the period from February through May.

3. The loan can be repaid during the year, with all suppliers paid and with sufficient cash left to retire the balance of the estimated income tax liability.

4. The company has adequate security to justify loans:

   a. Government Development Agency—first mortgage on the new building

   b. Bank—accounts receivable and inventories.

Cost of Sales Statement

The cost-of-sales statement clearly reflects the seasonal factors inherent in the changing sales pattern and the company's productivity and vacation cycle. Insurance and property taxes (lines 5 and 8) are level throughout the year. Material purchases (line 2) reflect the inventory buildup during the first four months of the year, and the seasonal factor clearly shows up in the summer months (lines 3, 4, 6 and 9). Direct labor and related factory overhead costs are substantially lower, while maintenance and repair costs (line 7) are definitely higher during this same period, when maintenance will least interfere with production.

Cost of sales per month is one of the principal factors in projecting monthly earnings. The amount of detailed support needed for this projection is dependent on the extent of product lines and mix implicit in the sales projections.

Earnings Statement

The earnings statement shows the rising and falling curve of monthly sales expected for the year, with the heaviest month, July, more than twice the lightest month, January. Because the cost of sales is staggered, the gross profit spread is even larger, ranging from $3,167 in January to $19,267 in July. Selling expenses rise dramatically from May through October, and administrative expenses are highest from March through September because of heavy interest charges.

Earnings for the year are healthy, with gross profit running at the targeted 12.5% and net profit before and after taxes running about 6% and 3.5%, respectively.

Cash-Flow Statement

When you calculate the timing of a bank loan, the cash-flow statement is critical. Because of the heavy expenses entailed in the inventory buildup to meet summer sales, Relentless Pursuits would be seriously short without the bank loans (line 3). Even with the advances, the company will be cash poor in February and very tight through November.

The statement serves both as an indicator of the right timing for the bank loan and as an early warning to management that if actual performance were to fall below the expected level, the company might have problems.

So the cash-flow statement is one of the principal management tools for monitoring operations during the year. For example, if sales for a given month—or cumulative sales through that month—are significantly below budget, management is forewarned that receivables for the following months will be lower than anticipated and that liquidity problems may develop unless action is taken. Management has adequate lead times because the assumption on customer payments realistically provides for a pattern of staggered payment ranging from 30 to 90 days. Similarly, any substantial departure from the anticipated pattern of cash collections may be a warning. The modest cash balances anticipated for April through November indicate that the company would be wise to establish a procedure each month to review its collections and the collectibility of outstanding balances for possible follow-up.

Balance Sheet

Breaking down the balance sheet for each month rounds out the picture for both management and lenders. Alone, it shows an increase in total assets from the opening balance of $243,700 to the closing December balance of $377,700. In conjunction with other statements, it provides both a broad and a detailed profile of projected company operations for the year, enabling both management and lenders to assess the year's prospects clearly and confidently.

Monthly Reporting of Actual Performance

In the case of Relentless Pursuits, monthly reports show a reasonable relationship between budget and actual results, but in July significant differences suggest the need for operational changes. To illustrate this, Exhibits E, F, G and H present the results of operations for the seven months ended in July.

These exhibits show that sales had been 3% higher than anticipated before July, but that that month's sales themselves were considerably underforecast. The deficiency resulted from external factors, primarily a number of strikes in a highly industrialized area that reduced consumer purchasing power. Although raw material purchases declined in July, when sales decreases became apparent, the purchase slowdown did not match the sales decrease. As a result, the owner-manager must consider action to deal with the effects of decreased accounts receivable, increased inventories, increased bank loans and decreased payables.

Since inventories are now excessive, purchasing according to projections would worsen the imbalance. Prolonged strike activity will impair the ability of his market to sustain both projected buying and payment levels. And the Company's cash collections in August and September will be automatically lower because of the reduced sales level already experienced.

While cash flow for the year to date has been in step with the budget, the company must expect problems during August and September unless remedial action is taken. The ending cash balances for both August and

September in the original budget (Exhibit C) were small, and so, to avoid significant deficits for those months, management must cut back cash outlays. This may include cancellation of all purchases of raw materials for August, reducing inventories and payables by $41,500. Peak collections on receivables previously anticipated for August will not be realized. But the cancellation of August purchases, combined with moderate cutbacks of purchases in July, would reduce payments on raw material purchases by $8,400 in August and $33,925 in September.

Although the company may have some minor cash problems in August, prompt actions should restore stability by September. It should be noted here that, in the absence of a budgeting system, the company might well have observed the sales decline and considered some kind of remedial action. But the the owner-manager probably could not have responded as promptly and might have been dependent on a more drastic move—perhaps, drawing up an emergency analysis of his financial position, evaluating it, and then weighing what action might be required. From a practical viewpoint, the company could be enmeshed in serious financial problems before corrective measures could be taken.

Reviewing the actual results of operations (Exhibits E to H), we can see that other variances are not material (aside from the departure from the sales budget). Also the reasons for being off-course are not related to any chronic condition likely to influence future sales or cost expectations. Thus, preserving the basic budget with appropriate reservations about conditions influencing the summer months would be preferable to making budget revisions. Essentially, the budget must be seen for what it is—a practical guide to cash control.

INSTRUCTIONS FOR PREPARING PROJECTIONS

Objectives and Assumptions

First, develop and record the statement of business objectives. Then establish and record the assumptions on which the forecast is based.

Cost of Sales and Operating Statements

Follow these procedures to project the monthly cost of sales, earnings, cash flow and balance:

1. Estimate net sales by month (Exhibit B, line 1).
2. Apply lead time information (assumptions) to establish monthly estimate of:

- Inventory levels required to service projected sales

- Production required to meet projected sales and inventory needs
- Raw material purchases needed to meet projected production needs

3. Estimate monthly inventory levels, considering period of inventory buildup to meet peak season sales (Exhibit A, lines 1 and 14).

4. Estimate overhead items and direct labor costs based on projected production schedule (Exhibit A, lines 3 to 12; note assumptions made for payment of expenses).

5. Compute monthly cost of sales figure (Exhibit A, line 15) using most recent gross profit information available. If gross profit tends to fluctuate by season due to sales mix, then monthly percentage will be needed.

6. Add line 14 to line 15 to arrive at line 13. This permits computation of line 2, monthly material purchases, completing Exhibit A (line 13 minus lines 1, 3, and 12).

7. Review Exhibit A noting reasonableness of expense allocations and material content of cost of sales compared to previous experience and in light of current projections.

8. Giving consideration to time of payments, transfer appropriate information on Exhibit A to Exhibits C and D as follows:

Item	Exhibit A	Exhibit C	Exhibit D
Inventory	Line 14	—	Line 3
Direct labor	Line 3	Line 6	—
Insurance	Line 5	Line 7	—
Property taxes	Line 8	Line 8	—
Fuel, utilities, maintenance and repairs, trucks and employee benefits	Lines 4, 6, 7, 9 & 10	Line 9	—

9. Complete lines 4 through 15 of Exhibit B by estimating selling and administrative expenses.

10. Prepare first month's estimate for following items:

Exhibit B
Line 16   Interest expense
Line 20   Income taxes

Exhibit C
Line 15   Interest payments
Line 17   Income taxes

11. Again, considering timing of payments, transfer appropriate information on Exhibit B to Exhibit C as follows:

Item	Exhibit B	Exhibit C
Salaries (selling)	Line 4	Line 10
Salaries (administrative)	Line 10	Line 14
Professional fees	Line 11	Line 12
Business taxes and licenses	Line 14	Line 13
Printing and postage	Line 12	} Line 16
Telephone and telegraph	Line 13	
Sundry	Line 15	
Interest	Line 16	Line 15

12. Applying appropriate assumptions for receipts and disbursements (Exhibit C), allocate information for lines 1, 2, 5, 10, 11, 18, and 19.

13. Complete Exhibit B for month and determine if it appears realistic in light of all assumptions. Then complete Exhibit C, estimating either bank loans (line 3) or bank repayments (line 20).

14. Complete first month for following items on Exhibit D:

Line 1	Cash
Line 2	Accounts receivable
Line 10	Bank loans
Line 13	Income taxes
Line 16	Shareholders' advances
Line 17	Capital stock

15. Compute net fixed assets, line 8, by deducting depreciation expense (Exhibit A, line 11 and Exhibit B, line 8), and adding plant additions, if any (Exhibit C, line 18).

16. Compute accounts payable, line 11, from Exhibits A and C.

17. Compute long-term debt balances, line 15, from Exhibit C, line 19.

18. Compute retained earnings, line 18, from Exhibit B.

19. Apply accrual accounting techniques used in cost of sales and earnings statements to expense payments of Exhibit C to compute line 4 and line 12.

20. Complete Exhibit D for first month and determine if it is reasonable in light of all assumptions.

21. Adjust first-month statements (above) as determined necessary.

22. Repeat procedure for each of remaining 11 months of year.

Relentless Pursuits Company
Projected Statement of Monthly Cost of Sales
For the year ending December 31

	January $	February $	March $	April $	May $	June $	July $	August $	September $	October $	November $	December $	Total $	
1 INVENTORY—BEGINNING OF MONTH	68,000	110,000	157,000	189,000	210,000	195,400	178,200	148,600	120,200	99,300	92,800	85,400	68,000	1
2 MATERIAL PURCHASES	78,500	86,400	72,200	62,300	38,100	49,900	49,600	41,500	32,600	42,800	37,100	36,200	627,200	2
3 DIRECT LABOR FACTORY OVERHEAD	3,600	3,600	3,600	3,600	3,000	1,100	1,100	1,100	1,100	3,000	3,600	3,600	32,000	3
4 Fuel	800	800	800	600	400	200	200	200	400	600	800	800	6,600	4
5 Insurance	400	400	400	400	400	400	400	400	400	400	400	400	4,800	5
6 Utilities	1,500	1,500	1,500	1,500	1,000	900	900	900	1,900	1,000	1,500	1,500	14,600	6
7 Maintenance and repairs	300	300	300	300	1,500	2,000	2,000	2,000	1,500	600	300	300	11,400	7
8 Property taxes	633	633	633	633	633	633	633	633	633	633	633	637	7,600	8
9 Trucks	400	400	400	400	200	50	50	50	150	300	400	400	3,200	9
10 Employee benefits	50	50	50	950	50	50	50	50	50	950	50	50	2,400	10
11 Depreciation	1,350	1,350	1,350	1,350	1,800	1,800	1,800	1,800	1,850	1,850	1,850	1,850	20,000	11
12	5,433	5,433	5,433	6,133	5,983	6,033	6,033	6,033	5,883	6,333	5,933	5,937	70,600	12
13	155,533	205,433	238,233	261,033	257,083	252,433	234,933	197,233	159,783	151,433	139,433	131,137	797,800	13
14 INVENTORY—END OF MONTH	110,000	157,000	189,000	210,000	195,400	178,200	148,600	120,200	99,300	92,800	85,400	80,200	80,200	14
15 COST OF SALES	45,533	48,433	49,233	51,033	61,683	74,233	86,333	77,033	60,483	58,633	54,033	50,937	717,600	15

Relentless Pursuits Company
Projected Statement of Monthly Earnings
For the year ending December 31

	January $	February $	March $	April $	May $	June $	July $	August $	September $	October $	November $	December $	Total $	
1 SALES	48,700	52,500	53,600	55,100	70,200	89,400	105,600	93,200	71,400	65,800	59,300	55,200	820,000	1
2 COST OF SALES	45,533	48,433	49,233	51,033	61,683	74,233	86,333	77,033	60,483	58,633	54,033	50,937	717,600	2
3 GROSS PROFIT	3,167	4,067	4,367	4,067	8,517	15,167	19,267	16,167	10,917	7,167	5,267	4,263	102,400	3
4 SELLING EXPENSES Salaries and commissions	900	900	900	900	1,200	1,600	1,800	1,600	1,200	1,200	900	900	14,000	4
5 Advertising	100	100	100	100	300	600	800	600	300	200	100	100	3,400	5
6 Delivery and freight	150	150	150	150	300	650	850	650	350	200	150	150	3,900	6
7 Automobile	150	150	150	150	150	150	150	150	150	150	150	150	1,800	7
8 Depreciation	100	100	100	100	100	100	100	100	100	100	100	100	1,200	8
9	1,400	1,400	1,400	1,400	2,050	3,100	3,700	3,100	2,100	1,850	1,400	1,400	24,300	9
ADMINISTRATIVE EXPENSES														
10 Salaries	900	900	900	900	900	900	900	900	900	900	900	900	10,800	10
11 Professional fees	125	125	125	125	125	125	125	125	125	125	125	125	1,500	11
12 Printing, postage, etc.	100	100	100	100	100	100	100	100	100	100	100	100	1,200	12
13 Telephone and telegraph	100	100	100	100	100	100	100	100	100	100	100	100	1,200	13
14 Business taxes and licenses	150	150	150	150	150	150	150	150	150	150	150	150	1,800	14
15 Sundry	50	50	50	50	50	150	150	150	150	150	50	50	1,200	15
16 Interest	200	575	1,090	1,555	1,705	1,665	1,620	1,400	1,080	860	750	700	13,200	16
17	1,625	2,000	2,515	2,980	3,230	3,190	3,145	2,925	2,605	2,385	2,175	2,125	30,900	17
18	3,025	3,400	3,915	4,380	5,280	6,290	6,845	6,025	4,705	4,235	3,575	3,525	55,200	18
19 NET PROFIT BEFORE TAXES	142	667	452	(313)	3,237	8,877	12,422	10,142	6,212	2,932	1,692	738	47,200	19
20 INCOME TAXES	50	233	158	(109)	1,133	3,107	4,348	3,550	2,174	1,026	592	258	16,520	20
21 NET PROFIT	92	434	294	(204)	2,104	5,770	8,074	6,592	4,038	1,906	1,100	480	30,680	21

Exhibit C

Relentless Pursuits Company
Projected Statement of Monthly Cash Flow
For the year ending December 31

	January $	February $	March $	April $	May $	June $	July $	August $	September $	October $	November $	December $	Total $	
CASH RECEIPTS														
Receivable	47,350	47,580	50,000	52,560	54,090	60,990	76,370	93,960	99,020	85,720	71,340	63,760	802,740	1
Mortgage loan	30,000	30,000	30,000	30,000	—	—	—	—	—	—	—	—	120,000	2
Bank loans	—	26,000	48,000	36,000	23,000	—	—	—	—	—	—	—	133,000	3
	77,350	103,580	128,000	118,560	77,090	60,990	76,370	93,960	99,020	85,720	71,340	63,760	1,055,740	4
CASH DISBURSEMENTS														
Raw material purchases	30,000	68,875	84,425	75,750	64,775	44,150	46,950	49,675	43,525	42,975	42,800	37,100	631,000	5
Direct labor	3,600	3,600	3,600	3,600	3,000	1,100	1,100	1,100	1,100	3,000	3,600	3,600	32,000	6
Factory overhead:														
insurance	—	—	—	—	—	—	4,800	—	—	—	—	—	4,800	7
property taxes	—	—	—	—	—	—	7,600	—	—	—	—	—	7,600	8
other, excluding depreciation	3,050	3,050	3,050	3,050	3,750	3,150	3,200	3,200	3,200	3,000	3,450	3,050	38,200	9
Selling expenses:														
salaries and commissions	900	900	900	900	1,200	1,600	1,800	1,600	1,200	1,200	900	900	14,000	10
other, excluding depreciation	400	400	400	400	400	750	1,400	1,800	1,400	800	550	400	9,100	11
Administrative expenses:														
professional fees	—	—	1,500	—	—	—	—	—	—	—	—	—	1,500	12
business taxes and licenses	—	—	—	1,800	—	—	—	—	—	—	—	—	1,800	13
salaries	900	900	900	900	900	900	900	900	900	900	900	900	10,800	14
interest	200	575	1,090	1,555	1,705	1,665	1,620	1,400	1,080	860	750	700	13,200	15
other	250	250	250	250	250	350	350	350	350	350	350	250	3,600	16
Income taxes	1,200	1,200	1,200	1,200	1,200	1,200	1,200	1,200	1,200	1,200	1,200	1,200	14,400	17
Plant addition	30,000	30,000	30,000	30,000	—	—	—	—	—	—	—	—	120,000	18
Long-term debt repay't	—	—	—	—	—	—	—	—	—	5,000	5,000	5,000	15,000	19
Bank repayment	—	—	—	—	—	6,000	6,000	32,000	45,000	27,000	12,000	5,000	133,000	20
	70,500	109,750	127,315	119,405	77,180	60,865	76,920	93,225	98,955	86,285	71,500	58,100	1,050,000	21
CASH OVER (SHORT)	6,850	(6,170)	685	(845)	(90)	125	(550)	735	65	(565)	(160)	5,660	5,740	22
CASH BALANCE— BEGINNING	—	6,850	680	1,365	520	430	555	5	740	805	240	80	12,270	23
CASH BALANCE— END	6,850	680	1,365	520	430	555	5	740	805	240	80	5,740	18,010	24
BANK LOAN—														
BEGINNING	—	—	26,000	74,000	110,000	133,000	127,000	121,000	89,000	44,000	17,000	5,000		25
Loan (repayments)	—	26,000	48,000	36,000	23,000	(6,000)	(6,000)	(32,000)	(45,000)	(27,000)	(12,000)	(5,000)		26
BANK LOAN—END	—	26,000	74,000	110,000	133,000	127,000	121,000	89,000	44,000	17,000	5,000	—	—	27
BANK SECURITY														
Accounts receivable	58,350	63,270	66,870	69,410	85,520	113,930	143,160	142,400	114,780	94,860	82,820	74,260		28
Inventories	110,000	157,000	189,000	210,000	195,400	178,200	148,600	120,200	99,300	92,800	85,400	80,200		29
	168,350	220,270	255,870	279,410	280,920	292,130	291,760	262,600	214,080	187,660	168,220	154,460		30

Relentless Pursuits Company
Projected Monthly Balance Sheets
For the year ending December 31

Exhibit D

	Opening Balance Sheet $	January $	February $	March $	April $	May $	June $	July $	August $	September $	October $	November $	December $	
CURRENT ASSETS														
1 Cash	—	6,850	680	1,365	520	430	555	5	740	805	240	80	5,740	1
2 Accounts receivable	57,000	58,350	63,270	66,870	69,410	85,520	113,930	143,160	142,400	114,780	94,860	82,820	74,260	2
3 Inventories	68,000	110,000	157,000	189,000	210,000	195,400	178,200	148,600	120,200	99,300	92,800	85,400	80,200	3
4 Prepaid expenses	—	—	—	1,125	2,200	1,925	1,650	6,544	5,236	3,928	2,620	1,312	—	4
5	125,000	175,200	220,950	258,360	282,130	283,275	294,335	298,309	268,576	218,813	190,520	169,612	160,200	5
FIXED ASSETS														
6 Costs	158,700	188,700	218,700	248,700	278,700	278,700	278,700	278,700	278,700	278,700	278,700	278,700	278,700	6
7 Accumulated depreciation	40,000	41,450	42,900	44,350	45,800	47,700	49,600	51,500	53,400	55,350	57,300	59,250	61,200	7
8	118,700	147,250	175,800	204,350	232,900	231,000	229,100	227,200	225,300	223,350	221,400	219,450	217,500	8
9	243,700	322,450	396,750	462,710	515,030	514,275	523,435	525,509	493,876	442,163	411,920	389,062	377,700	9
CURRENT LIABILITIES														
10 Bank loans	—	—	26,000	74,000	110,000	133,000	127,000	121,000	89,000	44,000	17,000	5,000	—	10
11 Accounts payable	40,000	88,500	106,025	93,800	80,350	53,675	59,425	62,075	53,900	42,975	42,800	37,100	36,200	11
12 Accrued liabilities	3,700	5,008	6,316	7,249	8,532	9,415	11,148	5,350	4,950	4,150	4,350	3,700	3,700	12
13 Income taxes	—	(1,150)	(2,117)	(3,159)	(4,468)	(4,535)	(2,628)	520	2,870	3,844	3,670	3,062	2,120	13
14	43,700	92,358	136,224	171,890	194,414	191,555	194,945	188,945	150,720	94,969	67,820	48,862	42,020	14
15 LONG-TERM DEBT	—	30,000	60,000	90,000	120,000	120,000	120,000	120,000	120,000	120,000	115,000	110,000	105,000	15
16 SHAREHOLDERS' ADVANCES	45,000	45,000	45,000	45,000	45,000	45,000	45,000	45,000	45,000	45,000	45,000	45,000	45,000	16
17 CAPITAL STOCK	5,000	5,000	5,000	5,000	5,000	5,000	5,000	5,000	5,000	5,000	5,000	5,000	5,000	17
18 RETAINED EARNINGS	150,000	150,092	150,526	150,820	150,616	152,720	158,490	166,564	173,156	177,194	179,100	180,200	180,680	18
19	243,700	322,450	396,750	462,710	515,030	514,275	523,435	525,509	493,876	442,163	411,920	389,062	377,700	19

Relentless Pursuits Company
Statement of Cost of Sales
For the seven months ending July 31

	Month				Year To Date			
	Projected $	Actual $	Difference Over (Under) $	Comments	Projected $	Actual $	Difference Over (Under) $	Comments
INVENTORY— BEGINNING OF PERIOD	178,200	181,700	3,500		68,000	68,000	—	
Material purchases	49,600	38,400	(11,200)	Down due to sales decrease.	437,000	440,900	3,900	Increased purchases due to increased sales; offset by July decrease.
Direct labor	1,100	900	(200)	Production down due to decreased sales and inventory buildup.	19,600	19,900	300	Increased production to meet increased sales prior to July.
Factory overhead:								
Fuel	200	200	—		3,800	3,650	(150)	Mild winter.
Insurance	400	450	50	Rate adjustment re new addition.	2,800	3,150	350	Rate adjustment re new addition.
Utilities	900	1,000	100	Increased power consumption because of heavy repairs.	8,800	9,050	250	Increased production to June plus July repairs.
Maintenance and repairs	2,000	2,600	600	Employee carelessness caused equipment burnout.	6,700	7,100	400	Fewer repairs during increased production to June.
Property taxes	633	667	34	Increased mill rate.	4,431	4,669	238	Increased mill rate.
Trucks	50	50	—		1,900	1,940	40	
Employee benefits	50	50	—		1,250	1,300	50	
Depreciation	1,800	1,800	—		10,800	10,800	—	
	6,033	6,817	784		40,481	41,659	1,178	
	234,933	227,817	(7,116)		565,081	570,459	5,378	
INVENTORY— END OF PERIOD	148,600	165,950	17,350	Sales volume down.	148,600	165,950	17,350	
COST OF SALES	86,333	61,867	(24,466)		416,481	404,509	(11,972)	

Relentless Pursuits Company
Statement of Earnings
For the seven months ending July 31

Exhibit F

	Month				Year To Date			
	Projected $	Actual $	Difference Over (Under) $	Comments	Projected $	Actual $	Difference Over (Under) $	Comments
SALES	105,600	72,200	(33,400)	Industrial community riddled with strikes; consumers have decreased buying power.	475,100	452,850	(22,250)	Sales volume up approximately 3% over projections prior to July.
COST OF SALES	86,333	61,867	(24,466)		416,481	404,509	(11,972)	
GROSS PROFIT	19,267	10,333	(8,934)		58,619	48,341	(10,278)	
SELLING EXPENSES								
Salaries and commissions	1,800	1,600	(200)	Decrease in sales.	8,200	8,190	(10)	Varies with sales.
Advertising	800	800	—		2,100	2,150	50	
Delivery and freight	850	750	(100)	Decrease in sales.	2,400	2,350	(50)	Varies with sales.
Automobile	150	150	—		1,050	1,075	25	
Depreciation	100	100	—		700	700	—	
	3,700	3,400	(300)		14,450	14,465	15	
ADMINISTRATIVE EXPENSES								
Salaries	900	900	—		6,300	6,300	—	
Professional fees	125	125	—		875	875	—	
Printing, postage, etc.	100	145	45	Increased postal rates.	700	845	145	Increased postal rates.
Telephone and telegraph	100	120	20		700	770	70	
Business taxes and licenses	150	150	—		1,050	1,050	—	
Sundry	150	180	30		650	730	80	
Interest	1,620	1,635	15	Higher loan balance.	8,410	8,460	50	Higher loan balance.
	3,145	3,255	110		18,685	19,030	345	
	6,845	6,655	(190)		33,135	33,495	360	
NET PROFIT BEFORE TAXES	12,422	3,678	(8,744)		25,484	14,846	(10,638)	
INCOME TAXES	4,348	1,287	(3,061)		8,920	5,196	(3,724)	
NET PROFIT	8,074	2,391	(5,683)		16,564	9,650	(6,914)	

Relentless Pursuits Company
Statement of Cash Flow
For the seven months ending July 31

Exhibit G

	Month Projected $	Month Actual $	Month Difference Over (Under) $	Month Comments	Year To Date Projected $	Year To Date Actual $	Year To Date Difference Over (Under) $	Year To Date Comments
CASH RECEIPTS								
Receivables	76,370	77,840	1,470	Increased sales to June.	388,940	397,380	8,440	Increased sales to June. July decrease will reflect in decreased collections in August and September.
Mortgage loan	—	—	—		120,000	120,000	—	
Bank loans	—	—	—		133,000	133,000	—	
	76,370	77,840	1,470		641,940	650,380	8,440	
CASH DISBURSEMENTS								
Raw material purchases	46,950	48,360	1,410	Increased purchases to June.	414,925	428,795	13,870	Increased purchases to June.
Direct labor	1,100	900	(200)		19,600	19,900	300	Refer to cost of sales.
Factory overhead:								
Insurance	4,800	5,400	(600)		4,800	5,400	600	Refer to cost of sales.
Property taxes	7,600	8,000	400		7,600	8,000	400	Refer to cost of sales.
Other, excluding depreciation	3,200	3,200	—		22,300	22,190	(110)	
Selling expenses:								
Salaries and commissions	1,800	1,600	(200)		8,200	8,190	(10)	
Other, excluding depreciation	1,400	1,400	—		4,150	4,275	125	
Administrative expenses:								
Professional fees	—	—	—		1,500	1,500	—	
Business taxes and licenses								
Salaries	900	900	—		1,800	1,800	—	
Interest	1,620	1,635	15		6,300	6,300	—	
Other	350	350	—		8,410	8,460	50	
Income taxes	1,200	1,200	—		1,950	2,150	200	
Plant addition	—	—	—		8,400	8,400	—	
Long-term repayment	—	—	—		120,000	120,000	—	
Bank repayment	6,000	4,000	(2,000)	Increased purchases.	12,000	5,000	(7,000)	Increased purchases.
	76,920	76,945	25		641,935	650,360	8,425	
CASH OVER (SHORT)	(550)	895	1,445		5	20	15	
CASH BALANCE—BEGINNING	555	(875)	(1,430)		—	—	—	
CASH BALANCE—END	5	20	15		5	20	15	
BANK LOAN—BEGINNING	127,000	132,000	5,000		121,000	128,000	7,000	
Loan (repayments)	(6,000)	(4,000)	2,000		—	—	—	
BANK LOAN—END	121,000	128,000	7,000		121,000	128,000	7,000	

Relentless Pursuits Company
Balance Sheet
For the seven months ending July 31

Exhibit H

	Projected $	Actual $	Difference Over (Under) $	Comments
CURRENT ASSETS				
Cash	5	20	15	
Accounts receivable	143,160	112,470	(30,690)	July sales down.
Inventories	148,600	165,950	17,350	Purchases slowdown did not match sales decrease.
Prepaid expenses	6,544	6,956	412	
	298,309	285,396	(12,913)	
FIXED ASSETS				
Cost	278,700	278,700	—	
Accumulated depreciation	51,500	51,500	—	
	227,200	227,200	—	
	525,509	512,596	(12,913)	
CURRENT LIABILITIES				
Bank loans	121,000	128,000	7,000	
Accounts payable	62,075	52,105	(9,970)	Purchases slowed because of sales decrease.
Accrued liabilities	5,350	6,045	695	
Income taxes	520	(3,204)	(3,724)	Decreased earnings.
	188,945	182,946	(5,999)	
LONG-TERM DEBT	120,000	120,000	—	
SHAREHOLDERS' ADVANCES	45,000	45,000	—	
CAPITAL STOCK	5,000	5,000	—	
RETAINED EARNINGS . .	166,564	159,650	(6,914)	
	525,509	512,596	(12,913)	

INDEX

A

Accounting system
  account titles, arrangement of, 40-41
  adequacy of financial information, 41-42
  contra accounts, establishment of, 41
  general ledger, set-up and posting, 39-40
  policy for, 39
Accounts payable
  C.O.D. purchases, guidelines for, 185-186
  control devices, 183
  freight bills, processing of, 184-185
  policy for, 183
  posting invoices to accounts payable subledger,
    186-187
  reconciliation of A/P subledger to A/P general
    ledger, 187
  reconciliation to suppliers' records, 187
  recording invoice in voucher register, 186
  review of debit balances in accounts payable, 187
  review of discrepancies, 187
  voucher package, 183-184
  voucher sheet, 188
Accounts receivable
  accounts receivable subsidiary ledger, reconciliation
    of, 84
  adjustments, posting of, 83
  credit balances, review of, 84
  cutoffs, review of, 84
  policy for, 83
  posting as independent function, 83
  sales invoices, posting of, 83
  timely identification of errors, 83
Application controls, 11-14
  accuracy of input in, 12-13
  authorization of transactions in, 13
  completeness of input in, 11-12
  computer-generated data/transactions, accuracy of,
    14
  policy for, 11
  rejected transactions, handling of, 13-14
  updating, 14
Asset balances

investigation of discrepancies, 119
policy for, 119
preparation of reconciliations, 119
supervisory review, 119
Assets. *See* Capital asset disposal; Capital
  assets

B

Balance sheet, 297, 306
  consolidated balance sheet, 301
Bank reconciliations
  determining reconciliation items, 65-66
  policy for, 65
  preparation of, 65
  review of, 66
Bond discounts/premiums
  amortization schedule for, 213
  policy for, 213
  recording of, 213
Book value per share ratio, 315
Budget. *See* Three-way budget
Business ratios
  book value per share ratio, 315
  current ratio, 314
  days in inventory ratio, 313
  days in receivables ratio, 314
  debt to equity ratio, 313
  inventory turnover ratio, 313
  price-earnings ratio on common stock, 315
  quick (acid-test) ratio, 313
  receivables turnover ratio, 314
  return on assets ratio, 314
  return on net worth ratio, 314

C

Capital asset disposal
  disposal form, 161
  documentation of disposal, 159
  fully depreciated assets, 160
  recording disposal, 159-160

Capital assets
    comparing inventory to detailed records, 157
    identification/record of assets, 157
    policy for, 157
    resolution of differences, 158
Capital stock
    approval by board of directors, 245
    examination of unissued and retired certificates, 249
    issuance of certificates, 245-246
    issuance of stock when full payment received, 246
    maintaining evidence of transfer, 246
    maintaining stock journal, 247
    policy for, 245, 247, 249
    posting to general ledger accounts, 248
    reconciliation to general ledger, 249
    registrar reports, preparation of, 247-248
    review of discrepancies, 249
    transferability of certificates, 246
Cash flow statement, 308
    consolidated cash flow statement, 303
Cash management
    cash budgets, 52
    cash receipts, expediting of, 51-52
    collection practices, 52
    disbursements, deferral of, 52
    idle funds, maximizing returns on, 51
    policy for, 51
    short-term investment vehicles, 53
    See also Three-way budget
Cash receipts
    bank deposits, 56
    endorsement of checks, 55
    opening the mail, 55
    policy for, 55
    reconciliation of cash/checks to deposits, 56
    summarization of cash receipts, 56
Computer operations
    activity logs, 28-29
    back-up and recovery, 29-30
    correct data files, use of, 28
    job set-up and evaluation, 27-28
    operations schedule, 31
    operator actions, control of, 28
    operator incident log, 32
    policy for, 27
    scheduling, 27
    See also System/program implementation

Computer systems
    benefits of system, 320
    company features for computerization, 320
    consultants, use of, 327-328
    costs of system, 324-325
    evaluation of needs for system, 320-322
    installation process, 325-326
    proposals from suppliers, 323
    selection of system, 322
    service bureau, 324
    software, 323
    value of computer system, 319-320
Cost-flow methods
    consistent use of method, 95
    determining appropriate method, 95
    policy for, 95
    production costs, allocation of, 96
    standard costs and overhead, review of, 96
    variance, proration of, 96
    variance analysis, 96
Credit policies
    accounts receivable agings, 72
    collection of delinquent accounts, guidelines for, 72
    credit limit increases, 72
    customer credit check, 71-72
    establishing credit guidelines, 72
    policy for, 71
    security interest in items sold, 72
    segregation of duties, 71
Current ratio, 314
Customer purchase order
    credit department approvals, 74
    order log, 73
    policy for, 73
    prenumbered sales order forms, 73-74
    sales order form, 76
    sales order form as packing slip, 74
    sales order form as requisition for merchandise, 74
    shipping log, 77
    shipping log preparation, 75
Customer returns
    allowed allowances, 86
    conditions for allowances, 86
    credit memo, 86
    credit memo issuance, 85
    credit memo numerical sequence, review of, 86
    policy for, 85

returned goods, count and examination of, 85
separate check of mathematical accuracy, 86
valid but unprocessed claims, 86
written authorization, 85

D

Days in inventory ratio, 313
Days in receivables ratio, 314
Debt agreements
    original agreements, 205
    physical safety of, 205
    policy for, 205
Debt, assumption and authorization
    approval and agreement for, 203
    board of directors resolution, 203
    collateralization of debt, 203
    policy for, 203
Debt covenants
    frequency of checklist preparation, 217
    noncompliance with, 218
    policy for, 217
    review checklist, 217
Debt payments
    by other methods, 212
    policy for, 211
    principal and interest components, 211
    through general ledger distribution, 211-212
Debt records
    bond price fluctuations, 208
    cash received in exchange for debt, 207
    policy for, 207
    property/plant/equipment in exchange for debt,
        207-208
Debt summary
    activity summary, 215
    comparison to general ledger, 215-216
    current portion of debt, 216
    policy for, 215
Debt to equity ratio, 313
Depreciation. See Property/plant/equipment
    depreciation
Disbursements from bank accounts
    cash disbursements, summarization of, 59
    check control log, 61
        maintenance of, 59
    check request form, 60

check signing, 58
disbursement of checks, 58
policy for, 57
preparation of checks and bank transfers, 57-58
supporting documentation, cancellation of, 58

F

Financial resource requirements
    bonds, 200-201
    installment/mortgage loans, 200
    long-term leases, 201
    notes payable, 199-200
    policy for, 199
Financial statements
    balance sheet, 297, 306
    cash flow statement, 299, 308
    consolidated balance sheet, 301
    consolidated cash flow statement, 303
    consolidated income statement, 302
    income statement, 298, 307
    schedule of cost of goods manufactured, 309
    schedule of cost of goods sold, 304
    schedule of general/administrative expenses, 305
    schedule of operating/administrative/general
        expenses, 300
    schedule of store expenses, 304
Forecasting of sales
    policy for, 93
    preparation of forecasts, 93
    production levels, review of, 94
    production volume, determination of, 93-94

G

General ledger
    authorization of entries, 45
    authorized vouchers, review of, 45
    close of income/expense items, 48
    documentation of entries not originating in journals,
        44
    documentation for journal vouchers, 45
    journal voucher, 46
    monthly activity, 43-44
    policy for, 43, 47
    reconciliations, 47

General Ledger *(cont.)*
    review of trial balance/reconciliation, 47-48
    set-up and posting, 39-40
    trial balance, preparation of, 47
Goods and services, needs determination
    limitation on purchases through imprest funds, 167
    methods for, 165-166
    policy for, 165
    requisition form, 168
    requisitions for goods/services, preparation of,
        166-167
    requisitions for plant/property/equipment, 167
    requisitions for specialized services, 167
Goods and services, receipt and acceptance
    communication between departments, 176
    comparing receiving log to receiving reports, 178
    discrepancies, review of, 178
    documentation, filed in receiving/sent to
        purchasing, 177
    inspection of materials, 175-176
    policy for, 175
    receiving control log, 181
    receiving report, 179-180
    receiving request, preparation of, 176-177
    storing/controlling of goods, 177-178
See also Return of goods

I

Imprest and similar funds, 63-64
    disbursement of funds, 63
    payment of payroll through imprest funds, 64
    policy for, 63
    post activity to general ledger, 64
    reimbursement of imprest funds, 63
    summarization of disbursements, 63
Income statement, 298, 307
    consolidated income statement, 302
Interest expense accruals
    amortization schedule for, 209
    policy for, 209
Internal control system, 5-8
    accuracy in, 5-6
    completeness in, 6
    determination of validity procedures, 7-8
    maintenance controls, 6
    physical security, 7

    policy for, 5
    validation in, 5
Inventory. *See* Periodic physical inventory;
        Perpetual inventory; Inventory
        control; Inventory obsolescence
Inventory control
    authorization for movement of inventory, 97-98
    custodial control, 97
    independent check of transferred items, 98
    materials requisition form, 99
    policy for, 97
    regularly scheduled physical counts, reconciliation
        of, 98
    written procedures for, 97
Inventory obsolescence
    disposal of obsolete inventory, 109
    policy for, 109
    revalue inventory to net realizable gain, 109
Inventory turnover ratio, 313
Investments
    access control log, 134
    account balances agreed to bank/broker statements,
        126-127
    authorization of investment vehicles, 124-125
    common/preferred stock, 137
    control log, 134
    dividend earnings worksheet, 140
    equity method of accounting, 141
    gain/loss calculation worksheet, 131
    held by authorized agent, 133
    income schedule, 138
    interest income, 137
    interest income worksheet, 139
    investee corporation earnings, 141-142
    investment control log, 129
    investment file, preparation of, 134-135
    investment purchases, 125
    investment sales, 125-126
    personnel action form, 128
    physical safeguards, 134
    policy for, 123, 124
    premium/discount on bonds and notes receivable,
        138
    purchase/sale authorization form, 130
    reconciliation of accounts, 126
    results reports, 126
    safekeeping receipt, 133

safekeeping receipt form, 136
sales gain or loss, 126
sales proceeds, 126
storage facility, 134
summary schedule, 138
types of investment vehicles, 123-124
valuation of marketable equity securities, 138

L

Liabilities, accrued
list of expenses, 221
measurement of reasons for, 222
monthly reconciliations, 223
policy for, 221, 223
recording accrual, 222
review of account balance, 222
review of discrepancies, 223
supervisory review of reconciliation, 223

O

Orders, placement of
approval limit schedule, 172
approval of review, 171
guidelines, establishment of, 169-170
multiple-copy purchase order forms, 171
personnel for, 169
policy for, 169
prenumbered purchase orders, preparation of, 170
purchase commitments, entering into, 170
purchase order, 173
review for accuracy, 170
unmatched commitments, review of, 171

P

Payroll calculation
independent payroll calculation, 237
payroll authorization, 237
payroll compared to control totals, 237
policy for, 237
time cards, 237
See also Wages/salaries
Payroll deduction
independent check of, 241

policy for, 241
recording of, 241
review of deductions to third parties, 241
Periodic physical inventory
concurrent physical inventories, 103-104
control of, 103
frequent period physical counts, 104-105
held in warehouses, 105
identification of inventory ownership, 105
indirect materials and supplies inventory, 106
inventory not on premises, 105
inventory tag, 108
policy for, 103
reconciliation of physical to perpetual inventory, 106-107
Perpetual inventory
approval for posting to general ledger, 111
general ledger adjustments, 111
not used inventory, 101
opening balance inventory, 101
physical count summary, review of, 111
policy for, 101, 111
Personnel
compensation and evaluation, 228
new employees, 227
personnel action form, 231
policy for, 227
vacation/sick pay, 228
Prepaid expenses
amortization periods and rates, 116
asset register, 117
journal entries, preparation of, 116
maintenance of asset register, 115-116
policy for, 115
review of income invoices to ensure prepayment, 115
Price-earnings ratio on common stock, 315
Program maintenance
cataloging, 23
cataloging authorization form, 25
internally maintained applications, 21-22
policy for, 21
service request form, 24
vendor maintained packages, 22-23
Property/plant/equipment
appropriation request, approval of, 146
appropriations request form, 147

Property/plant/equipment*(cont.)*
    approval of capital budgeting, 146
    capital asset purchase authorization, 146
    long-term lease or purchase, 146
    policy for, 145
Property/plant/equipment depreciation
    determination of method for, 156
    determination of useful life, 155-156
    policy for, 155
    tax deferrals through accelerated depreciation, 156
Property/plant/equipment records
    capitalization of expenditures while building, 150-151
    depreciable assets net acquisition costs, 150
    detailed fixed asset ledgers, maintenance of, 149-150
    expenditures, capitalization vs. expense, 151
    fixed asset ledger, 152-153
    investigation/resolution of differences, 150
    policy for, 149
    posting to detailed ledger, 150
    purchase price variances, review of, 149
    receipt and identification of capital assets, 149
    reconciliation to general ledger, 150
Purchase cut-off
    policy for, 195
    procedures for, 195-196
Purchase order. *See* Customer purchase order

Q

Quick (acid-test) ratio, 313

R

Ratios. *See* Business ratios
Receivables turnover ratio, 314
Return of goods
    debit memo, 190-191, 194
    invoice price compared to debit memo, 191
    materials rejection report, 193
    policy for, 189
    receipt of credit memo from vendor, 192
    rejection of material report, 189-190
    review of discrepancies, 192
    review of rejection reports, 191-192

    review of unmatched credit memo, 192
    shipping goods back to vendor, 190
    See also Customer returns
Return on assets ratio, 314
Return on net worth ratio, 314
Revenue recognition
    invoicing procedures, 79
    policy for, 79
    prenumbered invoices, 79
    sales invoice form, 81
    sales journal posting to general ledger, 80
    sales journal review, 79
    sales journal summarization, 80
    shipping log, review of, 80
Revenues (miscellaneous)
    barter transactions, 90
    deferred income, 89-90
    policy for, 89
    rental income, 89
    royalties, 89

S

Security
    access request form, 36
    administration of, 34
    dial-up access, 34
    high-level programming languages, use of, 35
    normal access controls, bypassing, 35
    off-line storage, custody of data, 34-35
    output, 35
    physical access, 34
    physical security, 7
    policy for, 33
    security policy, development of, 33
    system access controls, 33
System/program implementation, 15-19
    cataloging, 17
    data conversion, 18
    documentation in, 17-18
    documentation index, 19
    new data, set-up of, 18
    policy for, 15
    programming standards, 16
    system design, 16
    system development, management of, 15-16

testing procedures, 16-17
vendor-supplied packages, 16
See also Computer operations

T

Three-way budget
approach to, 333
assumptions in, 336-337
balance sheet, 339
benefits of, 332
as cash control guide, 331-332
cash-flow statement, 338-339
and changing conditions, 335-336
components of, 333
corrective action and, 335
cost-of-sales statement, 338
earnings statement, 338
first budget, preparation of, 333-334
monthly performance reporting, 339-340
objectives of, 336
performance monitoring for, 334-335
preparation guidelines, 337

projections, preparation of, 340-350
review and revision of budget, 335
Timekeeping
maintenance of records, 233
overtime approval, 233
policy for, 233
reconciliation of payroll to supporting records, 233
time card, 235
time sheet, 236

W

Wages/salaries
authorization of changes, 229
changes in payroll data, 229
comparing check endorsements to signatures on file, 239
comparison of payroll data to personnel files, 230
distribution of payroll, 239
policy for, 229, 239
receipt log, cash payments, 239
reconciliation of payroll bank accounts, 240
unclaimed payroll checks, 239